The
Day
War
Broke
Out

Jacky Hyams is a freelance journalist, editor, columnist and author with over twenty-five years' experience in writing for mass-market magazines and newspapers in the UK and Australia.

A Londoner who has spent many years travelling, her feature-writing career was launched in Sydney, Australia, where she wrote extensively for the *Sydney Morning Herald*, *Sun Herald*, *Cosmopolitan*, *Rolling Stone*, *Good Housekeeping*, *New Idea*, *Clio* and *The Australian Women's Weekly*. Returning to London, she spent several years as a women's magazine editor on *Bella Magazine*, followed by six years as a weekly columnist on the London *Evening Standard*.

Her memoir, *Bombsites & Lollipops: My 1950s East End Childhood*, and its follow-up, *White Boots & Miniskirts: A True Story of Life in the Swinging Sixties*, were published in 2011 and 2013 respectively, both by John Blake Publishing. She is also the author of The *Real Downton Abbey*, a brief guide to the Edwardian era (John Blake Publishing, 2011) and *The Female Few*, a study of the women Spitfire pilots of the Air Transport Auxiliary, while her most recent books are *Bomb Girls: Britain's Secret Army: The Munitions Women of World War II* and *Frances Kray: The Tragic Bride* (both John Blake Publishing, 2013 and 2014).

JACKY HYAMS

The
Day
War
Broke
Out

Untold true stories
of how British families faced the
Second World War together

JOHN BLAKE

Published by John Blake Publishing,
The Plaza,
535 Kings Road,
Chelsea Harbour,
London SW10 0SZ

www.facebook.com/johnblakebooks
twitter.com/jblakebooks

First published in paperback in 2019

Paperback ISBN: 978-1-78946-126-8
Ebook ISBN: 978-1-78946-146-6

Design by www.envydesign.co.uk

Printed and bound in Great Britain by Clays Ltd, Elcograf S.p.A

1 3 5 7 9 10 8 6 4 2

MIX
Paper from
responsible sources
FSC® C018072

John Blake Publishing is an imprint of Bonnier Books UK

CONTENTS

ACKNOWLEDGEMENTS

WARMEST THANKS TO THE EVER-HELPFUL STAFF AT THE JUBILEE Library, Brighton, Hove Library, the research teams at The Keep Archives in Falmer, and in London the Imperial War Museum and Westminster Reference Library.

Many thanks too for the valuable assistance given by Chris McCooey, Lyn Hall, Eva Merrill, Frank Mee, Arian, Ariette and Christian Everett, Katie Avagh and family, Irene Watts, Liverpool Museums, *Derby Evening Telegraph* (now the *Derby Telegraph*) and the Mass Observation Archive.

Maureen Hone, Vera Barber, Christine Haig, Jean Ledger, Eileen Weston, Philip Gunyon, Pat Thorne, John Blake of the Barking and District Historical Society, and Selma Montford also gave valuable assistance. Others whose collaboration was greatly appreciated include Pat Cryer (of the website www.1900s.org.uk), Pat Thorne, Alexandra Wilde,

THE DAY WAR BROKE OUT

Simon Stabler of *Best of British*/Yesterday Remembered and
Dr Kath Smith of Remembering the Past, Tyneside.

AUTHORS NOTES

Before 1971 the pound was divided into 20 shillings (s).

One shilling was made up of 12 pennies (d).

A pound was made up of 240 pennies.

A guinea was worth 21 shillings, or 1 pound and 1 shilling (£1 1s 0d).

I have given prices and sums of money in the original pre-decimal currency, which was replaced in February 1971.

In order to calculate today's value of any original price quoted, the National Archives has a very useful website with a currency converter.: http://www.nationalarchives.gov.uk/currency-converter. As a general rule of thumb, £1 in 1939 was worth about £40 in today's currency.

INTRODUCTION

THE DAY WAR BROKE OUT

How did the nation react to the news that war had just been declared? How did ordinary families across Britain, many still living with the haunting consequences of the previous world war, deal with the arrival of such a devastating pronouncement?

There are times when it may seem that every aspect, military or otherwise, of the events of the Second World War has been explored, examined and revisited time and time again in every medium you care to think of. Each year on Remembrance Sunday the country takes time out to revisit it all – to honour the contribution of British and Commonwealth men and women, military and civilian, in the two world wars – and the role they continue to play in conflicts across the globe. It is perhaps the one unifying point in any year when due homage is paid to victory and loss, to powerful memory and the significance of the country's history – and, in the First and Second World Wars, to how millions from countries across the world had joined with Britain to fight. Yet for me, one question above all has long dominated my thoughts when we stop to look back each year. Who were we, as a nation, on the day war broke out, 3 September 1939?

What was day-to-day life like for the civilian population of Britain, a country whose very empire at the time spanned an incredible 25 per cent of the globe, yet was still a small island where divisions of class and geography dominated almost everything? There is much to discover about Britain in 1939. In the first instance, the 1930s have mostly been viewed by history in a negative light, dominated as those years were by a global Depression and high unemployment in many parts of the country. To say that ordinary working people then did not have very much in terms of spending power, possessions or all the other accoutrements of the consumer society we now inhabit is not an exaggeration. By today's standards families were, mostly, quite poor. There was very little welfare from an unsympathetic state to prop them up. No NHS either. If you had a job, even if it was poorly paid, you were all right. You might be on the edge, but you'd survive. Just.

Families in the 1930s did not experience the same kind of mobility we take for granted either. There was a public transport network and there were, by today's standards, small numbers of cars and motorbikes on the road. But you needed to be quite well-to-do even to own a car. Jumping on a plane? Again, unknown to ordinary people, strictly for the very well-heeled. Yet what is fascinating about the era is that the very beginnings of a consumer society, similar to that of today, had started to emerge in Britain a few years before 1939.

Home ownership, especially in the city suburbs, had started to become a reality for some. Council-house building and the planned demolition of many slum areas by local authorities was under way. The extreme popularity of Hollywood movies had started to exert its powerful influence on millions, especially young women who could copy the fashions and hairstyles of the movie stars of the day, often sitting at home making their own versions of what they'd seen on the big screen. Television, of course, was barely in its infancy. So the huge popularity of cinema held sway – even through the war years and the bombing raids. Tickets to a movie palace were, after all, affordable for everyone, even children. From 1937 to 1940 a standard ticket cost just 10d (slightly over 4p).

One hugely important aspect of life in 1939 emerged not long after war was declared. Sending thousands of inner-city children off to the country, when it was believed that there would be huge bombing raids – including the use of poison gas – against city inhabitants virtually hours after war was declared, brought an important awareness of the huge variations in living standards according to income and class.

As I've mentioned, mobility for many was limited, especially those trapped in poverty. Yet even those more affluent middle-class households in the rural areas who had agreed to take in evacuee children were taken aback at the poverty and deprivation they encountered when these children, many from inner-city slums, were sent to live in their homes. This awareness of 'how the other half lived' would eventually take shape to bring reform of general living standards. Yet, although progression had slowly started to take shape with the commencement of the Beveridge report, it would be a long time before benefits were felt by the ordinary working folk of the United Kingdom.

In 1939, what still mattered very much were family cohesion and a pattern or routine to everyday living which has long gone. Today, churchgoing in Britain is at a record low. Yet Sundays then were for regular church attendance for most – frequently followed by the traditional Sunday lunch.

Men, in the main, were the breadwinners, women mostly stayed home and kept house. This way of life would be rent asunder by wartime, conscription and the eventual call-up of women when millions of them started working in paid employment for the war effort. Perhaps the true, understated importance of that warm day in September 1939 was that it was pivotal, marking a point where a process of huge, irreversible change would begin for the country and its people.

INTRODUCTION

This was a world without numerous television channels, fast food chains, credit cards, drones or instant messaging. Courtship meant going to a dance and letting a young man walk you home. Marriage was for life – divorce was rare, scandalous, and mainly the province of the wealthy. Access to a telephone meant the public phone box in a nearby street. Cosmetic enhancement meant a new lipstick, not a series of Botox treatments. Taking the temperature of ordinary lives in Britain on 3 September 1939 – and in the times before and after that day – is a surprising exercise. Some of what follows on these pages might sound quite shocking to twenty-first-century ears. Much of it, though, tells us that human nature itself can, at times, be strongly resistant to conditioning or environment. Determination, pluck, stoicism and a long-lost sense of community all had a part to play. Virtually every aspect of people's lives was about to be taken over by the state on the day war began. Today, of course, society would question such a bold step. Back then, it was mostly accepted. People grumbled, but in the main they simply got on with it. Perhaps the experiences of the previous war had saddened or soured many. Yet the instinct to survive, as ever, took over.

Finally, it was left to Frank Mee, one of the contributors to this book, a man who had lived through the story, to point out, with the wisdom of years, the truth of it all: in reviewing those all-important times, we can only hope and pray that neither we nor our families ever find ourselves facing such a situation again.

1

COUNTDOWN TO CATASTROPHE

MY MUM AND DAD WERE IN THE MIDST OF THE CROWD THAT night near the London Stock Exchange. A *Daily Express* photographer had been sent out onto the City streets to capture the moment, the instant-reaction shot as the people in the crowd scanned the newspapers.

I have a print of that black-and-white photo hanging on my wall, Mum smiling for the camera amid a sea of men's suiting, Dad, bespectacled, startled, a bit confused: twenty-somethings frozen in time, caught up in the historic moment.

The date was 30 September 1938.

IT IS PEACE, the headlines screamed, NO WAR WITH GERMANY.

Many were already convinced by then that war was imminent. But on that September night, Britain's Prime

Minister, Neville Chamberlain, had flown back from Munich after his third meeting with German Chancellor, Adolf Hitler, waving an important piece of paper, a non-aggression pact with Germany. Hitler had been readying to invade Czechoslovakia. Now, thanks to Chamberlain's diplomatic efforts, he had agreed to desist.

The bit of paper, the PM told the cheering crowds, 'was symbolic of the desire of our two peoples never to go to war with each other again.'

'Peace for our time,' he said that night.

'Yes, but how long is "our time"?' came the cynical response.

Perhaps understandably, some people clung to the hope that this was genuine, here was a last chance for peace. Others who had watched events in Germany in the last few years with growing alarm saw the Munich fiasco for what it was: a last-ditch diplomatic attempt to stave off the inevitable, a way of buying urgently needed time for both sides to prepare for war. Germany had openly rearmed while Britain's defences were in a parlous state. Preparations and planning for war, a shade too tentative until then, would now have to be accelerated with all speed.

Adolf Hitler's terrifying ambitions for war and domination of Europe had grown increasingly apparent not long after he and the Nazi Party came to power in Germany in 1933.

Hitler had never come to terms with Germany's defeat in the First World War and believed that the Treaty of

Versailles, the 1919 peace accord that ended the state of war between Germany and the Allied Powers, was grossly unfair: Germany had been stripped of territories, population and overseas colonies. He wanted the return of the territories that had belonged to Germany before the First World War. To this end, in March 1936, he sent his troops to reoccupy the Rhineland, a buffer zone between Germany and France which had been demilitarised after the First World War. Germany had been forbidden to station troops there. Hitler's aggressive move was in direct contravention of the Treaty of Versailles.

Unprepared for war, and despite vociferous diplomatic protests, neither France nor Britain took any action to halt or reverse Hitler's remilitarisation of the Rhineland. France had considered mobilisation but wanted British co-operation, yet, due to Britain's adamance regarding their policy of appeasement of Germany, Britain was unwilling to engage.

Elsewhere in Europe that year, further war clouds gathered. Italian Fascist dictator Benito Mussolini had waged and won war in Abyssinia (now Ethiopia). Afterwards, Germany and Italy formed a coalition, the Rome–Berlin Axis, linking the two Fascist countries.

In July 1936, the Spanish Civil War erupted, as Fascist General Franco attempted to seize power in Spain from the elected Republican government. One million lives would be lost in the war until the Republicans finally surrendered in March 1939, and Franco remained the dictator of

Spain until his death in 1975. To a considerable extent, the war had served as a testing ground for German and Soviet Russian military readiness, especially aircraft and tanks, with German armour and elements of the Luftwaffe (air force) supporting the Nationalists, and Russian forces operating on the Republican side; Italian forces also served in support of Franco.

Emboldened since his reoccupation of the Rhineland, Hitler's territorial ambitions rapidly expanded. He insisted the German people needed *Lebensraum* (living space) in the vast farming areas of Central and Eastern Europe, areas which could feed Germany and its peoples. This meant Hitler seizing even more territories.

In March 1938, Hitler annexed Austria into the German Reich, a move known as the Anschluss (the union or link-up). A few months later, the German Army was mobilised.

'Peace was dying,' wrote American war correspondent Virginia Cowles. 'Everyone in their hearts knew it.'

The tinderbox that would eventually lead to disaster was Czechoslovakia, then a country of many different ethnic groups formed after the First World War from part of the Austro-Hungarian Empire, which had been dissolved when war ended in 1918. Hitler wanted to annex an area in the north and west of the country called the Sudetenland, where three million German-speaking people lived.

Secretly, during a visit to Germany, Chamberlain had agreed that the Sudeten Germans could be separated from Czechoslovakia. Appeasement, i.e. diplomatic efforts to maintain peace even in the face of Hitler's aggression, was still, even then, the official policy for Britain's political class. Then, on Chamberlain's second visit to Germany on 22 September 1938, Hitler upped the ante with an advanced timetable for the handover of the Sudetenland and claims for more Czech territory. One week later, Chamberlain returned in triumph from his third visit to Germany, waving the ill-fated piece of paper.

Officially, at least, Chamberlain believed in the so-called peace treaty but essentially the idea was to avoid war with Germany through diplomacy until Britain had rearmed – despite any lesser compromises that might be involved. Yet when Hitler broke his Munich promises and occupied the rest of Czechoslovakia in March 1939, diplomacy and appeasement no longer held sway. The brief respite did give Britain time to build up defences and start a programme of rearmament. By then, Chamberlain acknowledged that Hitler was likely to seize Poland. In March 1939 France and Britain drew up an Anglo-French agreement, guaranteeing assistance to Poland, should Nazi Germany attack the country. Five months later came the words everyone had hoped would never be spoken: 'This country is at war with Germany.'

But why was Britain so 'lamentably unprepared' for war, as Winston Churchill later admitted? Why did the preparation for war only accelerate just a year before hostilities broke out?

Public opinion had much to do with the political

appeasement policy. Put simply, the politicians knew all too well that the people did not want another world war – the first one was still very firmly entrenched in the public consciousness.

Twenty years after the end of the First World War, 'the war to end all wars', when nearly a million lives of those within Britain and throughout the empire had been sacrificed in a four-year conflict (which eventually claimed sixteen million lives across the world), the idea of a second war against Germany was a shocking prospect for Britain's 47,760,000 inhabitants. Few families in Britain had not faced the many wartime hardships and losses. These were not restricted to the battlefields: more than 5,000 bombs were dropped by airships and aeroplanes in towns across Britain in the First World War, resulting in casualties of 1,413 killed and 3,409 injured, leading many to believe that there was little defence from bombardment from the air. As Harold Macmillan – British Prime Minister from 1957–63 – recorded in his memoirs; 'We thought of air warfare in 1938 as people think of nuclear power today.' Yet government spending on rearmament had not been a priority, thanks, in part to post-First World War economic depression and high unemployment in parts of the UK.

After Hitler took power, Germany became openly engaged in rearming, preparing for conflict. Britain had watched – and still hoped against hope that such conflict could never happen. Winston Churchill, then a backbench Conservative MP, spoke out against the German rearmament frequently. At the time, these warnings went largely unheeded.

Politically, too, there had been a deepening mood of gloom and unease among the public throughout 1936. This was the year of the Jarrow Crusade, when 200 men from the former shipbuilding town in County Durham, where nearly 70 per cent of the workforce was unemployed, had marched on London. Though unemployment had been falling since 1932, the national average was still 18 per cent; successive governments had attempted solutions – but failed. Another march held in October 1936 led to riots in London's East End when Sir Oswald Mosley and his Fascist Blackshirts paraded through the predominantly Jewish area to clash with anti-Fascists. Then, at the end of the year, the constitutional crisis caused by the marriage of the then King Edward VIII to the divorced American Wallis Simpson, which led to the King's abdication broadcast in December 1936, further heightened public unease.

Yet if the Munich fiasco was a key turning point for Britain's war planning, the subsequent events of November 1938 underlined the stark reality to anyone who still doubted Nazi aggression as reports of Kristallnacht (literally, 'crystal night', but generally translated as 'the Night of Broken Glass') started to come in.

This was a huge public attack, an act of Nazi violence against Jews across Germany, Austria and the Sudetenland during which 269 synagogues and 1,000 Jewish shops and homes were ransacked and set alight, windows of Jewish-owned buildings were smashed, Jewish homes, hospitals and schools destroyed, with hundreds killed and 30,000 arrested and sent off to concentration camps. The world looked on aghast at this officially sanctioned violence carried out on an unprecedented and truly frightening scale. Anti-war proponents could no longer ignore the ugly facts: Germany was internationally dangerous.

As if this wasn't frightening enough, the British authorities were convinced that a second war with Germany would open with a huge air attack on the country – an attack which would, in all likelihood, occur within a matter of hours of war being declared. It was thought that in the space of two weeks 600,000 people would be killed by any initial German bombing attacks, and twice as many injured.

London, it was believed, would be the main target. In the event, flat-pack cardboard coffins would be required since supplies of wood could not meet the anticipated demand. There might be mass burials. Moreover, the threat of poison gas attacks on civilians, following the use of different types of poison gas (by both sides) in the trenches during the First World War, also had to be taken very seriously indeed. This was a hideous prospect since mustard gas left survivors blind or at the very least with severely damaged lungs. The combination of air bombardment and poison-gas attacks, blinding, burning and tearing out the lungs of civilians led, not surprisingly, to fears that there could be panic on the streets.

For some time it had all seemed unthinkable; now it seemed to be edging its way towards a fearful kind of reality.

It was readily understood that a second war would partly be conducted by air. Since early 1935, with the establishment of the new German air force, the Luftwaffe (the Treaty of Versailles had forbidden Germany from maintaining an air force or submarine fleet, and reduced its army to a maximum 100,000 soldiers, and its navy to just six ships), Britain had witnessed Germany's ambitious plans to rearm and build up its air power. Until this point the Treaty of Versailles had forbidden Germany from maintaining an air force or submarine fleet, and reduced its army to a maximum 100,000 soldiers, and its navy to just six ships. Yet British future planning for the likelihood of enemy air attacks had been tentative, to say the least. Discussions on air-raid precautions (ARP) had taken place as far back as 1924, but it wasn't until July 1935 that local authorities in Britain had been urged by the government to prepare ARP plans.

The Air Raid Precautions Act, passed in 1937, formally required local authorities to start planning for government approval of their plans to protect civilians in the event of air attack. Yet progress in this direction was erratic at first: some local authorities simply didn't believe that war was likely to happen.

A number of plans for home defence had been drawn up, too – early in 1938, for instance, blackout trials, where homes and streets were temporarily blacked out to lessen the likelihood of successful bombing raids, had been attempted in Leeds and Nottingham. Yet it was the September '38 Munich crisis that propelled Britain's authorities to escalate, with all due urgency, the country's planning for conflict: war now became inevitable.

Pre-Munich, in March 1938, the Home Secretary of the time, Sir Samuel Hoare, had made an historic broadcast: 'If the emergency arose, I know you would come in your hundreds of thousands,' he said, making an appeal for volunteers to become air-raid wardens. Similar appeals were also published in the press, asking for volunteers over the age of thirty to join the ARP services as air-raid wardens, rescue workers and first-aid and ambulance workers.

Similarly, thousands of volunteer Army reservists had already signed up for the Territorial Army, and units trained alongside regular Army formations in summer camps during 1938 and 1939.

Within months, the appeals and publicity drive bore fruit: thousands, including large numbers of women, came forward to sign up as ARP volunteers, many on a part-time basis. These ARP wardens would play many grim roles: organising the distribution of gas masks, checking provision of shelters and ensuring blackout regulations were carried out. The part they played would become central in wartime Britain, as would that of the Auxiliary Fire Service (AFS), also set up that year to expand the peacetime fire brigades.

In May 1938, the Women's Voluntary Service (now known as the Royal Voluntary Service) was formed, initially to help women into the ARP movement, to assist civilians during and after air raids, and to help with the evacuation and billeting of urban children to the countryside. Government plans for large-scale evacuation of large towns and cities had acknowledged the need for evacuation planning; how this was to be organised had yet to be publicly set out.

The unofficial motto of the WVS, 'We never say no', characterised an important voluntary organisation which grew from 300,000 members in 1939 to over one million women, whose practical and organisational efforts would develop and expand into providing help in virtually every aspect of life in wartime Britain.

Historically, during the First World War, women had been engaged in paid work: 1,600,000 women were employed in 'men's jobs' like bus driving or as post office clerks as well as more traditional women's jobs like teaching or nursing, while many others worked in munitions factories.

Nonetheless, any kind of official conscription or call-up for women, even in 1938 with war looming, still remained highly controversial: the belief that a woman's place was firmly in the home continued to hold sway — until the exigencies of wartime with its demanding labour shortages took precedence and conscription for women in the armed forces became legal in 1941. Yet it would be the volunteering women, like those of the WVS, who would form much of the backbone of what became known as the Home Front, the mobilisation of civilians to support the war effort.

By the autumn of 1938, war planning was evident to all: sandbags to protect public buildings were ordered by the thousand. Huge trenches were dug in parks and playing fields (for people to take cover in in the event of an air raid) and thirty-eight million gas masks were ordered by the government, produced by a firm in Lancashire. These were distributed, free of charge, at various assembly points – usually schools – in late September, following a huge public campaign by poster, car loudspeakers and announcements at football matches, cinemas and churches to encourage everyone to equip themselves with a mask. Small children were equipped with Mickey Mouse gas masks and the very young were issued with a 'baby-bag' which could be fitted over an infant's head and shoulders.

At the same time, ARP volunteers, including those from the WVS, were being trained in procedures for dealing with gas casualties.

Air-raid shelters were built, many designed to be distributed free to low-income families for self-assembly in their gardens. This type of garden shelter was known as the Anderson shelter, named after Sir John Anderson (Home Secretary from September 1939–October 1940 and in charge of air-raid preparations) – a somewhat flimsy and damp form of protection from bombing raids. Three and a half million were produced. In the end, they did help save lives, but they were unpopular, mainly because their use in cold, damp weather made for a very uncomfortable experience. (In 1939 it was announced that those with an income of more than £250 a year had to pay a small amount for such a shelter.)

Larger shelters were planned, too. In a prescient move, in January 1939, Croydon Borough Council approved the conversion of a car park into a huge shelter housing 30,000 people at a cost of £300,000. (Croydon, to the south of London, with its factories, warehouses and what was then Britain's only international airport, as well as its proximity to RAF airfields in the South-East, was heavily bombed in the years ahead.)

As ARP precautions were finalised, detailed planning for the mass evacuation of children developed. By the end of September 1938, the government published its plans for the assisted evacuation of an estimated two million people from London, a quarter of them schoolchildren. Many families started to make their own private arrangements to evacuate the main cities and many courting couples rushed to marry – although this would escalate to record numbers the following summer. Those who recalled food shortages in the First World War even started to buy and hoard food. Aircraft production increased alongside a huge campaign to recruit all types of civil defence volunteers across the country.

In London, newspaper reports showed people invading the shops to buy blackout material to make coverings for windows at night. Every window in every home would have to be completely covered half an hour before sunset each night, not to be reopened until thirty minutes before sunrise. Volunteer local wardens would be responsible for patrolling the streets to ensure blackout rules were followed to the letter. There would be fines for breaching these rules.

Even cigarette manufacturers joined in the public-awareness campaign. Cigarette cards, placed inside packets of cigarettes and usually depicting Hollywood stars, famous sportsmen or historical figures, were hugely popular collectible items at the time. Bristol manufacturer W. D. & H. O. Wills – makers of the famous Woodbine cigarettes – started to include cards depicting civilian first-aid groups, running with stretchers, rescuing those injured by bombing raids.

The preparations, though eleventh hour, were wholly justified. In March 1939, the false dawn of Chamberlain's little piece of paper was revealed for what it was: Hitler contemptuously stuck two fingers up to British diplomacy and the Munich Agreement and marched his troops into Prague. He had already made territorial demands on the Baltic port of Danzig (now Gdańsk), part of Poland, claiming this rightfully belonged to Germany. (Under the Treaty of Versailles, Danzig and some two hundred surrounding towns and villages, the inhabitants of which were mainly German, had been declared a free city, in effect a semi-autonomous city-state, separate both from Germany and the newly independent Poland. The Treaty also guaranteed the 'Polish Corridor' to Danzig, which separated Germany's West Prussia from East Prussia.)

Two months later, plans for limited conscription in Britain were under way: 240,000 single men between the ages of twenty and twenty-two registered in June to undertake six months' military training. Exceptions to all conscription would be those working in 'reserved' occupations – jobs that were crucial to the war effort. 'Reserved' jobs included doctors, police, teachers, railway workers and those employed in coal mining, shipbuilding and engineering-related professions and trades.

In July 1939, the Civil Defence Act enabled faster progress to be made in the implementation of many wartime plans. Employers with more than thirty workers were now required to organise ARP training, while those with a workforce of more than fifty based in a large city or danger area had to provide a form of air-raid shelter for their employees.

By August, the annual British holiday season had been completely overshadowed by the threat of war. Naturally, families hesitated about heading off to the seaside or to country beauty spots in this situation. But for many people, common sense prevailed, thinking, 'Well, it might be our last good holiday before war breaks out,' so they opted to take the holiday. The announcement that petrol would be rationed if war broke out was a sobering reality check, though.

That August of 1939 was one of the warmest and driest on

record. But when the news came through on 23 August that Germany and the Soviet Union had signed a non-aggression pact, it was clear that Poland was painfully exposed, on both sides, to powerful enemies. As a consequence, Britain signed a treaty of alliance with Poland.

Within twenty-four hours of the news of the Nazi–Soviet Pact the Emergency Powers (Defence) Act was passed by both Houses of Parliament. This gave the British government wide powers to put the country on a war footing, creating regulations which affected almost every aspect of everyday life for population. Public safety, the defence of the realm, maintenance of public order and a host of other new wartime regulations were now in place.

'The peril of war is imminent but I still go on hoping,' Prime Minister Neville Chamberlain told the House of Commons.

Such hopes were in vain. All school teachers affected by evacuation plans were recalled from holiday to return to their posts. On 25 August, BBC Radio (or the 'wireless' as it was then known) started to broadcast special news bulletins at 10.30am and 1pm.

The rationing of food was now poised to be rolled out. Relatively limited food rationing had been introduced in the First World War at the beginning of 1918 and continued until 1920. By 1939, it was deemed a necessity in the event of war; three-quarters of food consumed in Britain came from abroad, even livestock were mainly dependent on imported foodstuffs.

Ration books for all were printed and ready, though food rationing would not come into effect until the following year. (The rationing of bacon, butter and sugar was introduced on 8 January 1940, followed by rationing of many other foodstuffs and, later on, of other items like clothing, fuel, soap and paper.)

Given the country's need to feed itself where possible, a major campaign was instituted to encourage the nation to be self-sufficient when it came to growing vegetables. Everyone in the country, men, women, schoolchildren, would be encouraged to 'Dig for Victory'.

That last week of August, the nation braced itself for war. The Admiralty closed the Mediterranean to British ships and British merchant shipping was ordered to leave Baltic waters. All passages by sea to New York and Canada were fully booked, and the cross-Channel boat trains were so crowded only passengers were permitted to travel on them; friends and relatives wishing to say goodbye could only do so at railway stations, rather than at the departure ports. The roads leading out of London and other large cities were crowded with streams of cars leaving the city for the countryside, piled high with luggage, prams, toys and other possessions.

Many of the cars were driven by women; applications for provisional driving licences had soared in the preceding few days.

In the early morning of 1 September 1939, under cover of darkness, German troops marched into Poland. Within hours, the capital, Warsaw, was being bombed. That same day, the planned evacuation of thousands of mothers and children from British cities began.

Toddlers clutching tiny cases and gas masks, with luggage labels pinned to their lapels, boarded buses, trains and, in some cases, boats, to make their way to the safety of the countryside, waved off by anxious parents. Photographs of these partings appeared in all the mass-circulation newspapers, creating a positive sense that the country was protecting its most vulnerable. These images would carry huge impact down the years.

That night, two days before Britain's formal declaration of war, the blackout went into effect throughout the country and many cinemas, theatres, clubs and places of entertainment were closed. (Most would, in fact, reopen after the declaration of war.)

Television broadcasting was shut down – the government was concerned that the VHF transmissions would act as a beacon for enemy aircraft homing in on London. In fact, in 1939, very few owned a television set – around 20,000 in London – but those who were watching discovered in the middle of a programme that the signal had been switched off, without warning. It would not be switched back on again until 1946.

An entire nation held its breath – and waited. The telephone system (still relatively new) nearly ground to a halt because of the volume of calls, the exhausted operators taking several hours to put through what were known then as trunk calls (long-distance calls within the same country) from London to provincial cities. The armed forces were mobilised. Police leave was cancelled. Driving tests were suspended. Bus services were cut to save fuel. Banks were closed for one day but reopened afterwards. In London, newspaper articles advised women to keep a reserve stock of food. Not many rushed to comply as they had done after Munich – such behaviour might seem unpatriotic. The Treasury withdrew support for sterling, allowing it to fall against the US dollar to conserve British gold stocks.

Big hospitals in London like St Thomas's began to clear their wards where possible, sending convalescents or patients with minor ailments home. Large London hospitals had already been told in mid-August to stop admitting patients unless the case was an emergency. Plans for hospital staff and patients to be moved by Green Line coach to bases in the country were now underway. Businesses finalised their preparations to move to safer areas, some preparing to send key personnel to the country.

Large retailers, too, made their own war preparations. In Manchester, the Kendal Milne department store was requisitioned for the Civil Service, with air-raid shelters created in the basement. (Trading did not cease, however: drapery and fashion departments were open to the public on two floors.) In Great Yarmouth, local department store Arnolds had its basement eventually converted into an emergency hospital, while trading continued on the floor above. Air-raid shelters were set up in basement areas of big London stores like Selfridges; some of these 'shop shelters' stored first-aid equipment and emergency food and water supplies.

That last warm weekend of the summer, all over the country people were praying for peace. Some churches remained open night and day, so that people might slip in at any time for a few moments of prayer. Britain's railway stations were jammed with travellers, many of them soldiers en route to join their units. A vast array of barrage balloons (large balloons anchored to the ground by cables as an obstacle to low-flying enemy aircraft) hovered in the sky above. Yet families continued to picnic in beauty spots, enjoying the last moments of their holiday. In so many ways, under such peaceful blue skies, it seemed somewhat unreal that the horror of war was about to be unleashed.

On 2 September, the temperature was over 70 degrees F (21 degrees C) for the fifth consecutive day. During the night, huge thunderstorms swept the country. In Portsmouth, a rumour started that the war had begun: four barrage balloons, struck by lightning, had caught fire, lighting up the sky. The last day of peacetime was over.

In London's Downing Street and Whitehall a huge patriotic crowd gathered, many staying through the night, mostly silent, waiting for news that did not come until the following morning.

Britain delivered its ultimatum to Germany, by letter, on the morning of 3 September at 9am. The letter stated that unless Germany agreed to withdraw its troops from Poland by 11am, Britain would 'fulfil its obligations to Poland'. The night before, the Prime Minister, Neville Chamberlain, still hesitated, hoping against hope that Hitler would heed the ultimatum and remove his troops from Poland.

Such hopes were in vain. An announcement was made on BBC Radio at 10am that the Prime Minister would be addressing the nation at 11.15am.

Across the country, people stopped what they were doing that bright morning: women still sewing their blackout curtains, men digging in their gardens or struggling to install home-made shelters, holidaymakers receiving the news by chance through landladies, open windows or on doorsteps, the many families who didn't own a wireless invited, for the first time, into their neighbours' living rooms, all assembling to hear the fateful words:

> This morning, the British Ambassador in Berlin handed the German government a final note, stating that unless we heard from them by eleven o'clock that they were prepared at once to withdraw their troops from Poland, a state of war would exist between us. I have to tell you now that no such undertaking has been received and that consequently, this country is at war with Germany.

The seventy-year-old Chamberlain sounded wrecked, truly exhausted. He had held out for peace, almost at any price, and believed Hitler's assurances – and been bitterly cheated by an implacable, relentless enemy. (He would resign in May 1940 during the disastrous Allied campaign in Norway, dying of colon cancer just six months later.)

Across Britain, millions struggled to absorb the news. The National Anthem was played just after Chamberlain's words had faded away; as was still their habit, many people rose to their feet for it.

Then, eight minutes after Chamberlain's broadcast, air-raid sirens were heard over London, parts of the Midlands and East Anglia for the first time. People rushed outside their homes: was this it? Some people even hastily donned their gas masks or ran into Anderson shelters they had already erected. What should they do? Yet it was the briefest of confusions. In fact, it was a totally false alarm, provoked by the sighting of a single French aircraft.

That same day, an Act of Parliament was passed, bringing in conscription for all men between the ages of eighteen and forty-one. Over 400,000 Territorial Army recruits were formally incorporated into the British Army. Britain's armed forces were just 500,000 strong before the declaration of war; by 1943, they would total 4.25million.

At 6pm that night, the people listened to King George VI broadcast to the nation:

For the second time in the lives of most of us we are at war. Over and over again we have tried to find a peaceful way out of the differences between ourselves and those who are now our enemies. But it has been in vain. We have been forced into a conflict. For we are called, with our allies, to meet the challenge of a principle which, if it were to prevail, would be fatal to any civilised order in the world.

It is to this high purpose that I now call my people at home and my peoples across the seas, who will make our cause their own. I ask them to stand calm and firm and united in this time of trial. The task will be hard. There may be dark days ahead and war can no longer be confined to the battlefield. But we can only do the right as we see the right and reverently commit our cause to God. If one and all we keep resolutely faithful to it, ready for whatever service or sacrifice it may demand then, with God's help, we shall prevail. May He bless us and keep us all.

Older women who had already lost loved ones, children, husbands or fiancés, brothers, in the previous war, understood the bitter reality of what lay ahead.

People of both sexes wept. Youngsters saw their parents cry for the first – or only – time, the children unable to comprehend the true meaning of the PM's words. Although some younger children envisaged war's onset as a welcome event, since persistent playground rumour claimed that if there was a war, all schools would be shut down indefinitely.

There was fear, anger and, of course, much bewilderment about what lay ahead. If there was any kind of mass panic, as feared, it went unrecorded anywhere in the broadcasts or newspapers of the time. That night, most went to bed with heavy hearts, some fearful of immediate attack, as all over the country searchlights scanned the night sky for the bombers. Yet the day itself ended peacefully.

Overall, the mood was apprehensive but calm, stoic, a quiet resolve, characteristic traits of the British which would surely help everyone through the very worst days and nights in the six years to come. Visitors to London from New York were amazed at the outward sangfroid of people on the streets of the city – in the heart of New York, by contrast, there was a fevered atmosphere when the news came through, even though at that stage, the US would remain neutral until December 1941, when the Japanese attack on Pearl Harbor catapulted the US into the Second World War.

The following day, 4 September, newspaper photos of workers in London, making their way as usual to the office, but with gas masks in their little boxes slung over their shoulders, underlined the theme of quiet British stoicism. Interestingly, preparations had already been made to deploy that British 'stiff upper lip' for use as wartime propaganda. The now well-known 'keep calm and carry on' morale-boosting poster had been designed by the Ministry of Information in July 1939. Yet for some reason, the poster itself was never sanctioned for wide use during the war (2.5 million copies were printed, yet stocks were eventually pulped as part of a wartime paper salvage campaign and it was only in 2000 that a surviving copy was discovered at a bookshop in Alnwick, Northumberland).

Yet one of the strangest events that followed the

announcement of the outbreak of war took place throughout that first week of September 1939. This was known as the massacre of cats and dogs. Millions of pets were put down – at the request of their owners. In London alone, 400,000 were killed humanely by vets and animal charities, though there were unofficial estimates that the number destroyed was closer to twice that.

This was not an order imposed by the government or, indeed, encouraged by the animal charities, rather a decision made by families who could not bear to consider the fate of their household pets if their homes were bombed or they themselves killed or if they could no longer feed their pets when rationing took precedence.

On London's streets, animal charities and vets' surgeries saw long queues of people waiting to hand over their much-loved cats and dogs. The incinerators at the People's Dispensary for Sick Animals (PDSA) could not cope with the numbers of corpses they received, eventually organising a pet cemetery in its grounds in East London.

The Royal Society for the Prevention of Cruelty to Animals (RSPCA), the world's oldest animal charity, confirmed afterwards: 'The work of destroying animals was continued, day and night, during the first week of the war.' The National Canine Defence League (now Dogs Trust) reported that so extensive was the slaughter of dogs, its supplies of chloroform had run out.

For all this, however, many families chose not to put down their pets. Devotion to domestic animals, as much a part of the British psyche as stoicism, was not disposed to disappear in wartime.

As for my own family witnesses to the historic moment of Chamberlain's return from Munich, I never did find out what my parents thought about it all – or even what they were doing in the crowd at the Stock Exchange that night of the disastrous announcement of 'peace for our time'. I knew something of their subsequent wartime history, of course, but I only chanced upon the press photo in a magazine article in 2009, and by then it was too late to ask them about that night.

Their register office marriage, like millions of others, was a rushed affair in 1940. I did not arrive until the war had ended. Yet through sheer good fortune, they and their immediate families survived the chaos and wreckage of what lay ahead: bearing witness to the courage and endurance of Britain's armed forces, the millions of volunteers on the Home Front 'doing their bit', fighting the civilian's war right the way through and beyond the darkest days of the Blitz and the bombing of Britain's cities.

During the Second World War, 400,000 British people lost their lives (including 60,000 civilians killed on British soil). Many other countries went on to endure devastation on an unprecedented global scale: an estimated fifty to sixty million lives were lost. Yet on that Indian summer's day in September, as the people of Britain made their way to church and back, sat down afterwards at the table to tuck into their Sunday roast, or listened to the radio again

(King George VI's broadcast to the nation that evening was much applauded. It had been a struggle for the shy King, whose stammer made every speech a huge ordeal, but he very much wanted to do it), Britain turned a page in its history – its future completely unknown.

The rhythm and routine of everyday life was poised to change completely: the state would have control of virtually every aspect of each citizen's life. Ahead lay rationing and shortages, years of separation, long hours of work for those in factories, hospitals and on the land or voluntarily helping the war effort.

For many men, the horrors of carnage amid the camaraderie would be seared into their memories for good. Families would be torn apart, loved ones injured, killed, or kept prisoner in spartan, and sometimes horrific, conditions. Homes would be wrecked by bombs, even grief would become commonplace. A few, in remote rural areas, would manage to live out the war years in relative peace, yet millions of lives would be affected in one way or another.

It would be six years before peace was finally declared in September 1945 [following the Japanese surrender] and another ten years beyond that before the country really started to recover and get back on its feet. Pre-war Britain, just as it was on that warm September morning in 1939 when peacetime slipped away, would be consigned to history. The phrase 'before the war' would fall into common parlance.

THE DAY WAR BROKE OUT

After the day war broke out, nothing would ever be quite the same again.

2

CHAOS

IMAGINE THIS: YOU ARE A SMALL CHILD, LIVING IN A CITY or large town, old enough to go to school. Your parents have been informed, by letter from the government, that in the possible event of war you and your siblings, if any, will need to be evacuated, for safety, to the countryside in small groups. If you have younger siblings, under five, your mother can accompany them.

This evacuation plan is not compulsory, it is for each family to decide what happens. But if you are over five years old and your parents want you to go, your mother will not be accompanying you – and she will not be told where you are being taken, or with whom you'll be living upon reaching your destination. It is an emotionally charged situation for everyone.

In 1938, the plan to evacuate certain areas of Britain

most likely to be bombed and separating large numbers of children from their parents to live with total strangers was an unprecedented event comparable to a military operation, should Britain's cities be subjected to a huge bombing attack from Germany.

The authorities believed that taking control before such a devastating event by planning to move large numbers away from the cities beforehand would save lives – and prevent mass panic.

Britain's initial large-scale evacuation plan, developed in the summer of 1938, by the Anderson Committee (its chairman was the former Governor of Bengal and Home Secretary, Sir John Anderson) looked at how the country would respond to the threat of prolonged and destructive aerial attack.

Public Information Leaflet No. 3, *Evacuation: Why and How*, sent out to households in July 1939, described it thus:

The scheme is entirely a voluntary one, but clearly the children will be much safer and happier away from the big cities where the danger will be greatest. There is room in the safe areas for these children; householders will have volunteered to provide it.

They have offered homes where the children will be made welcome. The schoolchildren will have their schoolteachers and other helpers with them and their schooling will continue. Do not hesitate to register your children if you live in a crowded area. Of course it means heartache to be separated from your children, but you can be quite sure they will be well looked after. That will relieve you of one anxiety at any rate.

The plan split the country into three zones: Evacuation, Neutral and Reception. The first Evacuation zones included Greater London, Birmingham, Manchester, Liverpool and Glasgow, with Reception areas, i.e. safe areas where the evacuees would be received, in rural places like Kent, East Anglia and Wales. Neutral areas were places that would neither send nor receive any evacuees.

The evacuees were split into four categories: school-age children, the elderly or infirm, pregnant women and mothers with babies or pre-school children (who were to be evacuated together).

In November 1938, the Anderson plan became the official government Evacuation Scheme. But where to house the evacuees? In the reception areas, accommodation would be needed to house an estimated 3,500,000 evacuees (England and Wales) and 400,000 in Scotland.

In January 1939, local authorities in the reception areas were asked to survey private homes to work out how many places – or billets, as they were called – would be available to house the evacuees.

The process of taking in families or unaccompanied children was called billeting. The word 'billet' generally means the living quarters in which a person is assigned to sleep; technically, it referred to a soldier's living quarters.

Yet the word was used in wartime either for those seeking a billet, i.e. wishing to rent a room in a family house, as well as for families outside the cities willing to take in a city evacuee or their family.

Calculating the numbers of available billets in reception or safe areas was a huge task. It involved surveying more than five million homes. Furthermore, billets were assessed in terms of availability rather than suitability.

Rural areas back then did not necessarily offer much in the way of home comforts: any heating usually came from a wood-burning fireplace and nearly half of homes in rural areas had no indoor lavatory – although deprived areas like London's East End could also be found lacking modern sanitation, for example, 90 per cent of homes in the Stepney area did not have one either.

More than one million rooms were privately reserved for people leaving the cities but not participating in the government evacuation scheme. These were the more affluent families more likely to make private arrangements to go to relatives, rent cottages, book hotels or boarding houses in areas like the West Country, rural Wales or Scotland.

It was compulsory for families with available billets in reception areas to host the inner-city evacuees in their homes, anyone refusing to do so faced the threat of a fine. Billeting allowances were paid to these householders taking in evacuees: initially, the allowances paid were 10 shillings and 6 pence a week for a single child and 8 shillings and 6 pence a week per child if more than one child was billeted. These allowances changed slightly, according to variations in the ages of evacuated children, during the war years.

There was also the issue of medical treatment: at a time when there was no free healthcare via the National Health Service (which was not established until after the war had ended), medical treatment had to be paid for. Arrangements were made with the medical profession that they would treat all evacuated children free of charge or, if necessary, treatment in a local hospital would be free.

Further government information, like leaflets for *The Protection of Your Home Against Air Raids*, were distributed to all households in July and August 1939, giving all details of the evacuation scheme. Additional public information leaflets, *Your Gas Mask* and *Masking Your Windows* followed. Distribution of these leaflets ensured all families would be coming to terms with the idea of possible attack. BBC Radio even broadcast an air-raid siren warning everyone to take shelter, so people could recognise the sound.

However, despite all efforts to encourage families to evacuate their children, the overall take-up for the scheme varied considerably. In Manchester, 75 per cent registered for evacuation. In London and Liverpool, 65 per cent agreed and in Glasgow 62 per cent, but in cities like Birmingham, Coventry and West Bromwich, the take-up was much lower, just 24 per cent of the local population.

On 31 August 1939, the government informed the local authorities in the evacuation areas that evacuation from the cities would commence the following day. BBC Radio public announcements informed listeners that even if anyone had not formally registered, they could still go. By then, many who had registered had changed their minds about sending their children away.

Joan Strange, from Worthing, West Sussex, was a physiotherapist in her thirties who became directly involved in helping Jewish people escaping from Central Europe and the Nazi regime in the late thirties. In January 1939, she helped establish the Worthing Refugee Committee. Her tireless efforts helping displaced persons and refugees in post-war Europe and South-East Asia continued throughout her life until her death in 1994.

Joan's wartime diary records the early effect of the evacuation in a West Sussex seaside town like Worthing, which had agreed to take in 13,000 evacuees.

1 SEPTEMBER

Wireless news at one o'clock told us that the London schoolchildren would be evacuated tomorrow. Terrible, as it makes war seem nearer. Surely it can't happen. It's dreadful to think that the 'victors' will be those who use most effectively the most diabolic instruments of death as quickly as possible.

The papers are very depressing – all the pictures are of soldiers, sandbags, ARP, city girls evacuating from their offices, guns, aeroplanes and so on. One neighbour has a £400 dug-out bomb-proof (?) shelter erected in his garden, disguised as a rockery but with two doors and two chimneys visible.

On 6 September, she wrote:

The first week of the war – it has been impossible to write daily for the last week as life has suddenly become very difficult under wartime conditions.

The blackouts have started, no one must show a glimmer of light anywhere. Cars have the merest glimmer left and have to be painted white in front, rear and on running boards – the roads have a white centre line and the kerbs whitened. Some food, especially sugar, is very scarce. Worthing, being a safe zone, has had over 10,000 evacuees from London billeted on the inhabitants. On Saturday, a friend and I helped billet some Bermondsey blind people. We both felt how terrible it was that so much money, time and trouble is taken to help these poor, old, ill, blind people while we send healthy, young, virile people to be killed. They were a really pathetic lot of people, mostly old (I took several who were over eighty), all dirty and several ill.

Worthing and the South Coast towns did not, of course, remain safe zones.

By spring 1940, with the increasing threat of invasion of England's South Coast, some 200,000 children, including the West Sussex evacuees, had to be evacuated or re-evacuated away from the coastal areas to safer locations.

Organising transport for the first wave of evacuation in September 1939 was a complicated logistical exercise. The Ministry of Transport and the railway companies estimated that transport by train, bus and in some instances, boat or ship, would be needed for nearly 3.5 million.

These were huge numbers. Effectively, the planners viewed the transportation of huge numbers as a military operation. Consequently, insufficient attention was given to what would happen when the evacuees arrived at their destination.

The planners over-estimated the numbers by more than 50 per cent. In the event, in the first three days of the official evacuation, less than 1.5 million were moved. The moving process involved teachers, local authority and railway staff, as well as 17,000 women from the WVS; these women were deployed to look after the evacuees and provided refreshments at railway stations and reception areas.

Families and teachers had been primed. Children needed to carry a kit: a handbag or case containing the child's gas mask, a change of underclothing, night clothes, house shoes or plimsolls, spare socks or stockings, toothbrush, comb, towel, soap and facecloth, handkerchiefs and, if possible, a warm coat or mackintosh. Furthermore, each child was required to bring a packet of food for the day. Poorer families certainly struggled with this, though billeting officers, teachers and volunteer workers did their best in the circumstances to improvise and provide help wherever possible.

Every child would have a luggage label pinned to their coat, bearing their name, school and evacuation authority. They remained unaware of where they were going, what they would be doing – and when they would be returning. It was, by anyone's standards, enormous upheaval for everyone involved.

While the evacuation plan succeeded on a logistical level, i.e. in transporting the 1.5 million without accident or injury, at the receiving end, it came close to chaos. Without the heroic efforts of the teachers and the volunteers accompanying the children, it could have been even worse.

The planners had focused on the logistics of moving large numbers of children and adults, but they had not fully understood the difficulties of placing unaccompanied children into billets.

Receiving families sometimes found it difficult to cope with the reality of accommodating a total stranger in their midst – or a mother with babies or toddlers who had no wish to be separated from them, even briefly.

'The women of England are depressed to death over the idea of the shared kitchen and the children unknown,' wrote Surrey housewife Constance Miles in her wartime diary on Wednesday, 30 August 1939.

Constance lived in Shere, a small village near Guildford in Surrey. The following day, on hearing that the evacuation of the children was due to commence, she wrote: 'Seventy children are due to arrive by buses here at 10.30. The evacuation notices are most inappropriately given out by BBC young men who know little what despair enters the hearts of various women expecting the strangers and afraid to have them.'

The confusion that often awaited the evacuated children and mothers once they had reached their destination stemmed partly from the fact that far fewer numbers than expected had turned up. Because of this, the carefully plotted train schedules for the first day of evacuation were thrown into total disarray. Many groups of children herded from schools to railway stations wound up boarding trains, irrespective of destination.

Such was the mix-up, reception areas expecting school-children found themselves greeting different groups, i.e. mothers with under-fives or pregnant women. Or school-children who had been carefully sorted into groups when their journey began were often split up en route if the journey involved a change of trains and ended by bus. In some places, children were taken away to billets by volunteer helpers before a list of names could even be taken. It would take a week or more before teachers who had started out travelling with groups of schoolchildren were then able to discover where their pupils had been taken. Families at home also had to wait to find out where their children were located.

Given that during early months of the war – dubbed 'the Phoney War' – were confusingly uneventful because the anticipated massive aerial attack did not take place at all, the many problems experienced by families or children finding billeting an unwelcoming or uncomfortable experience resulted in one thing: many just wanted to go home.

By Christmas 1939, over half of evacuees had done just that.

CHAOS

Logistically, Operation Pied Piper, as the large-scale movement of Britain's children away from the cities was known, had been a success in the first part. But for those who had been evacuated? Sometimes it was a very different story . . .

EVA'S STORY

Here is Londoner Eva Merrill's memory of evacuation:

Eva lived with her family in Haringey, North London. Eva, twelve, was the eldest of three. Her sister Dorothy was nine and their little brother, John, nearly two years old.

The Merrills were an ordinary family, living a happy, well-ordered life in the rented downstairs flat of a large terraced house. Eva's father, James, worked as a messenger in the City of London for a large firm of stockbrokers. He also had a part-time job on Sundays as a doorman at the BBC TV studios at Alexandra Palace. Eva recalled:

We didn't see a lot of him as he seemed to be always working, but we had a comfortable lifestyle and were in a far better financial position than many working-class families around us.

In 1938 I passed the scholarship and was a pupil at Hornsey County Grammar School. The following year, when Britain was planning for war in earnest and contingency plans were made for the evacuation of children from London and other cities, Dorothy and I brought letters home from our schools in the summer term of 1939, regarding possible evacuation.

Dad and Mum felt Dorothy and I should be evacuated so our names were put down at our respective schools. It was then announced that mothers with children under the age of five should also consider evacuation, taking their toddlers with them. As John was not quite two years old, Dad felt Mum should also be removed from possible danger, so they too registered for the evacuation programme.

Far from being nervous or worried about evacuation from their home, the Merrill girls cheerfully accepted the situation.

Most of our classmates had duly brought their forms back, all consenting to evacuation, rather like signing up for a mammoth school outing, Eva recalled.

Our school was issued with special songbooks in preparation, full of rousing and patriotic numbers which the music teacher rehearsed us in relentlessly. We were told that if and when we left London, we were to sing our heads off, there may be a war, but we were BRITISH and must never be downhearted. I can still remember us all bellowing out 'Land of Hope and Glory', 'Rule, Britannia!' and 'There'll Always Be An England' plus similar uplifting songs in the school hall, months before the war even started, just so that we should all be in good voice if that fateful day ever arrived.

Dad had been persuaded by his firm to join the Territorial Army in 1937, so along with several of his work colleagues, he had spent a week away at camp on Army manoeuvres each year. Mum thought it was all rather silly – after all, he was forty-two. She said they were like a lot of schoolboys playing games. However, Dad enjoyed the week or so away and as his employers paid his wages when he was on these jaunts, not too much notice was taken as to how he'd committed himself – nor did we realise the full implications.

By July 1939, Eva had completed her first year at grammar school and had settled in nicely. She was enjoying the new experience and coping with all the academic requirements. Dorothy too was doing well at junior school and toddler John was happy and contented.

We must have been more affluent that year for Dad had booked a two-week summer holiday for us at Winchelsea Beach, near Rye, in Sussex. This was to be in a disused railway coach, a great novelty – obviously a forerunner of caravan holidays. We travelled down to Winchelsea Beach by coach in early August and had a glorious ten days there. It was John's second birthday while we were there and I still have a photo of him, beaming away astride a large mock lion. It was a happy time for all of us, our parents were relaxed and carefree and the railway coach provided an endless source of amusement for Dorothy and I.

In the middle of the second week a telegram arrived, telling Mr Merrill to report to the Territorial Army barracks:

'He had to be there AT ONCE – he was already a day overdue because the letter telling him to report had gone to our home, causing some consternation all round. There we were in the middle of a lovely holiday and this bombshell arrives!'

The family packed up frantically and headed for home:

Dad was full of anxiety, fearing he would be arrested as a deserter, Mum furious at what she thought was the Territorial Army playing still more silly games. Us girls were somewhat resentful and upset at this sudden curtailment of our holiday, so it was a very unhappy little family that arrived back in London.

Once home, Dad picked up the travel warrant that was waiting for him on the doormat, along with instructions, and he rushed off to report to the army barracks. We were left to unpack our cases feeling thoroughly fed up and let down. No explanation was given as to why Dad had to go off in such a hurry, or how long it was for.

The days went by and there was still no letter or message from Mr Merrill.

We all grew very worried. Mum's money ran out and at last, in desperation, she contacted his employers. They were less than helpful, they told her they did not know where Dad was. They had merely been informed that he had been called up for the Army. As he was no longer an employee of theirs, there would be no wages forthcoming. Mum should contact the Army.

The next few days were difficult and bewildering for the family:

> I don't know how Mum got through or how she found money to feed us all. I think she probably pawned her engagement ring and watch with other bits and pieces. There was no welfare state in the 1930s and no agency one could go to for help. Food had to be paid for with hard cash and our gas supply was operated with a pre-payment slot meter. 'The Army' seemed a vague concept; how or where one set about finding information Mum had no idea, and nobody seemed able to offer any suggestions. It was all such a shock. One week we were a happy family on holiday, the next we were penniless on our own, with Dad spirited away into the British Army.
>
> Ten days passed before Dad arrived home resplendent in full Army uniform. Despite being blind as a bat without his glasses, not in very good health and forty-two years of age, he was now a private in the London Rifle Brigade. He'd also served in the First World War, from 1916 to 1918.

None of the men called up at this time had been allowed to contact their families or give any hint of the massive behind-the-scenes call-up.

Dad had been frantic with worry about us all, particularly

our financial situation, for he knew Mum had very little money when we came back from holiday in such a rush. But he had been powerless to do anything. Fortunately, he had brought an Army pay docket home with him, which Mum was able to cash, and a weekly allowance had been made out for Mum and us three children. This was about half what she had previously had coming in. His employers had earlier indicated to their staff when they persuaded them to join the Territorial Army should they ever be called up, the firm would consider making good any loss in wages. In the event, they declined to make good any such shortfall.

Dad spent a short leave with us and then returned to camp. He gave Mum his address but warned that he did not know how long he was to remain at this particular base as movement was likely. A day or so after Dad left, Mum received a letter saying we all had to meet at South Haringey Junior School on Friday, 1 September at 9.30am. We were all going to be evacuated.

There wasn't much time to get ready:

Mum hurriedly packed up for us, sent a note to Dad telling him of our impending departure and rushed around making the necessary domestic arrangements concerning the house. We were only allowed to take the minimum of luggage, nightwear and toilet articles, a change of clothing, a top coat and a second pair of shoes or boots. Each child had to have his own bag or case and, most essential of all, a gas mask. We'd been issued with these some time earlier. After the initial novelty of trying them out had worn off, they'd been left lying around in their cardboard boxes.

On Friday morning, 1 September, the Merrills joined the other children from South Haringey School and Hornsey County Grammar School in the playground.

Mums were there to wave their children off while others, like ours, were coming with us, complete with toddlers and babies. They tried to assemble us in some sort of order but with our party, it was difficult, Dorothy should have been with her junior school classmates, me with the Hornsey County group, Mum and John with the mother and toddler contingent. We were on three separate lists, it seemed. But Mum wasn't having that: she insisted we were all staying together, even though the officials assured her we'd all eventually arrive at the same place.

Outside the school, fleets of coaches (or charabancs as they were known then) were lined up to transport everyone.

Nobody knew where we were going. It was all a deadly secret, very hush-hush. Parents were virtually sending their children off into the unknown and there were many exhortations to 'write and let us know where you are' passed around. Why the parents could not be told on that day where their children were going, I do not know – many must have spent anxious days worrying about their children and waiting for information as to their whereabouts.

As Mum was so insistent that we four were to travel on the same coach, it was finally agreed that Dorothy and I should join a mother and toddler group. We waved our respective classmates onto their coaches and climbed onto a coach full of mothers and toddlers under five. Dorothy and I were the only school-age children on that coach – a fact that was to cause problems later on.

Eventually the coaches all set off in a convoy, with passengers and bystanders waving to each other excitedly. The mothers left behind looked on forlornly as the convoy increased speed and some of the children on the coaches started to become tearful. Eva noted: 'I thought I ought to be singing my head off – all that rehearsing at school – but none of the mums on our coach looked like breaking into song and I didn't feel like starting up on my own.'

Because there were so many young children on Eva's coach, the driver was obliged to make several comfort stops and eventually the inevitable happened: 'Our driver got left behind and completely lost track of the other coaches. The driver had not been told our final destination, he only knew it was somewhere on the Cambridge/Norfolk border.'

Nowadays, of course, the driver could have used his mobile phone or pager but, in 1939, such things were non-existent. There had been public telephone boxes in Britain since the 1920s, but most of the population did not even have a home telephone. All the driver could do was drive on.

The coach kept going and by mid-afternoon everyone was becoming increasingly frustrated. Toddlers and babies were tired and crying, mothers trying their best to cope with them while the harassed coach driver desperately tried to find his way. He kept stopping off at villages, asking for news of the other coaches – but nobody had seen any other coaches passing through. We went round and round, on and on, until eventually, he drew up at a large hall in the village of Upwell, near Wisbech in Cambridgeshire.

Waiting to meet the coach was a team of women from the Women's Royal Voluntary Service.

Great excitement greeted us. They had been told to expect some evacuees and having laid on urns of tea, cakes and sandwiches, they were becoming increasingly worried when no evacuees turned up. We were helped off the coach but before the first cup of tea passed anyone's lips, it was realised that we were not the expected party but a different group altogether.

There we stood, the mothers tired and gasping for a cup of tea while the good ladies of the WVS wondered what to do. They were reluctant to dispense their tea and cakes to this stray crowd when any minute now their bona fide evacuees could turn up also needing refreshment.

After much discussion and delay, Eva's group were all led into a hall and the food and tea made available to them.

We still did not know if we were staying, but eventually the powers that be decided as we were 'in situ', as it were, Upwell might as well have this lot rather than those planned for the village. Though it was a 'bird in the hand' situation, the officials at Upwell were not very pleased. They'd been told to expect schoolchildren and had canvassed the village for householders willing to take in a child. To be suddenly faced with mums, babies and toddlers was a very different proposition.

There then followed a heartbreaking and humiliating process while the villagers chose those they were willing to take into their homes.

We all sat around on long forms [benches], for hours it seemed, while villagers were encouraged to come and take their pick. They came in, in ones or twos, walked around us and looked us over. It was a most unnerving experience. We sat still and quiet, trying to look pleasant and acceptable, while weighing up our would-be hosts warily. After careful deliberation, one little family would be chosen – usually a mother with just one child. They would then be transported away by one of the WRVS women.

Our party was the largest with Mum and three children and the officials said we would have to be split up – nobody in the village could take us all. Mum did her solidarity bit again, said we were all staying together. She would not hear of us all being separated so we sat on while the room slowly emptied of mothers and children.

Before the Merrills had left, they had each been given a paper bag of 'iron rations' to be handed to their prospective householder.

Delving into this bag – which we had been expressly forbidden to do – I found an enormous bar of Cadbury's milk chocolate. I had never seen such a large bar before, we often had a small bar each at home but this was more mouth-watering than anything I'd ever seen. When we had our little bars, Dad always insisted we broke off a square at a time and daintily popped each morsel into our mouths. We were never allowed to munch at a whole bar, small though it may be. I'd always longed to bite and chomp at the total slab, and now here was this enormous bar in my hands. Behind cover of the bag and shielded by Mum, I surreptitiously peeled off the silver paper and took one huge bite.

Suddenly the air was rent by a thunderous shout from a hatchet-faced lady, who rushed over and snatched the chocolate from my hands. She proceeded to rant and rave at me for daring to open my bag, let alone actually start eating its contents – this appeared to be the ultimate sin. Mum was rounded on for letting me behave in this way, which left her quite bewildered.

Dorothy too was subjected to a lecture should she have the temerity to touch her bag, which reduced her to tears. Amid all the shouting and upset, little John wet himself and a large puddle slowly crept over the floor. Cowed and subdued, the family huddled together, feeling very isolated and wishing they had never left London.

'After the shock of this outburst had worn off,' Eva noted, 'Mum rallied and dug her heels in even more firmly, glaring at all and sundry and refusing to let either Dorothy or I be taken off without her. Eventually we were the only evacuees left in the room.'

Meanwhile, the officials bustled around, not quite knowing what to do, casting despairing glances at this awkward family.

At last one of the more diplomatic of their number came to Mum and told her she had found a household willing to take Dorothy and me and just across the road was another household who would accommodate Mum and John. This official said she would take us all to the first address so Mum could be sure Dorothy and I were all right. If she was satisfied, her own accommodation would be just opposite so we could be in constant touch with each other. I think Mum realised that we would never be placed together, so she reluctantly agreed to this arrangement.

Transport appeared and soon we arrived at a farmhouse to be greeted by a Mrs Watson, who showed Mum where Dorothy and I were to sleep. This was in the attic, a large, bare room under the eaves with discarded pieces of furniture and other bits of equipment stored around. There was an iron bedstead in the middle which had obviously been made up recently with fresh sheets and blankets. A rug had been placed beside it on the bare floorboards. Though not ideal, we were all very tired so Mum agreed to leave us there. She went off with the official to her own placement – which proved to be a very different proposition.

This was a small cottage occupied by an elderly couple. It was rather grubby and poorly furnished with no indoor sanitation or piped water. Neither gas nor electricity was laid on:

The old lady did not want to take in Mum and John, which given her circumstances, was hardly surprising. After an argument on the doorstep in which the official brought pressure to bear, it was found they had a spare bedroom with a bed in it, so they were obliged to take in an evacuee.

With very bad grace, Mrs Merrill and John were admitted.

We realised afterwards that neither the Watsons nor the old couple felt they were able to take in any evacuees, but because in each case they had spare sleeping accommodation, they were given little choice. This happened up and down the country and certainly did not help to foster good relationships between evacuee and host.

Dorothy and I were given something to eat and later on went up to bed, climbing the stairs, clutching a candle. It felt very strange lying in that bare attic room. We blew the candle out and settled down to sleep.

We soon became aware of scratching and other little noises, scampering feet and squeaks. It was mice, coming out from the woodwork and running round the room. We were terrified, but too scared to get out of bed and run downstairs in case the mice ran over our feet. We lay there clutching each other and wondering what we had let ourselves in for until finally, we fell asleep. So ended our first day of evacuation in still-peaceful Britain.

On that same day, 1 September, German forces attacked Poland by land, sea and air from three directions. No declaration of war had yet been made but the raids began at dawn and continued relentlessly. Britain and France could no longer stand by and ignore Poland's plight.

On Saturday morning, Dorothy and I were sent off after breakfast as Mrs Watson did not want us under her feet. We went over the road to Mum, who was struggling to get herself organised in very difficult conditions. The old lady did very little cooking and this had to be done on an old-fashioned kitchen range which needed a fire being lit in it. But as it was early September, the old couple flatly refused to start using their coal just yet.

They had a paraffin heater on which they boiled kettles of

water for tea or hot water for washing. They seemed mainly to live off cups of tea and biscuits, together with bread and cheese. Mum had plundered her bag of iron rations as there was little food in the house and had made a meal of sorts for John and herself. There was considerable tension between them and if Mum could have upped and left, she would have done.

We all went for a walk to explore the village, meeting up with others from our coach party. Exchanging views on our respective billets gave rise to much discussion, it was so different from the city life we knew. We all felt aimless and adrift and generally spent the day wandering around chatting. There was only one general store/post office and as far as we could tell, no public transport. We could find no trace of pupils from South Haringey School or Hornsey County – where they had finished up was a mystery. Some of the mothers had older children who had gone on the coach with their school group and they were quite understandably worried as to their children's whereabouts. There was no one to ask, the village hall was shut and the band of WVS ladies had disappeared. Mum was pleased she had insisted we all travel together, at least she knew where Dorothy and I were.

On Sunday, 3 September, Dorothy and Eva sat around the wireless in the Watsons' kitchen at 11.15am and listened as Neville Chamberlain broadcast to the nation, explaining that the country was now at war with Germany.

The adults all looked very solemn but Dorothy and I could not make out why nothing was happening. I don't know what we expected – soldiers marching through the streets, guns and tanks, perhaps? But there was no indication that the day was any different from the day before. After all the build-up over the few months before, we felt somewhat put out that it had finally arrived in this quiet and uneventful manner.

The rest of that weekend in Upwell passed reasonably enough for the two girls.

We soon learned that Mrs Watson, though civil enough, was not to be trifled with. She was a large and formidable woman with massive hips and an enormous bosom. She reminded me of the fat ladies depicted by Donald McGill in his saucy seaside postcards.

Mr Watson was a very quiet man and though not small in stature, he epitomised the meek husband, henpecked and totally dominated by his overbearing wife. It was his second marriage. His first wife had died; the second Mrs Watson was at least twenty years younger than him. A grown-up son from the first marriage still lived at home and worked with his father on the farm. Mr Watson's elderly father also lived with them. This frail old man was often the butt of Mrs Watson's tongue and he looked permanently miserable.

Eva had taken an instant dislike to Mrs Watson; the feeling was reciprocated. They were constantly at loggerheads.

CHAOS

I am sure she longed to give me a good clout from time to time, [but] she never quite dared to raise a hand to me. She was not over generous with the food, keeping her well-stocked walk-in pantry strictly out of bounds. It became a point of honour for me to creep in there every day and remove some biscuits or pieces of cake. These I would hide in our attic bedroom and share with Dorothy at night. It never occurred to me that the mice also enjoyed these offerings. Dorothy was always scared I would be caught and went through agonies on my behalf. A real bone of contention was our carrier bags of iron rations, which we had duly handed over when we first arrived. Despite all my promptings we never saw those bars of Cadbury's milk chocolate again – we suspected Mrs Watson had eaten them when we were in bed.

On Monday morning, Mrs Watson packed up sandwiches for Dorothy and me and sent us off to the village school. We had not expected this, but dutifully trailed up the road until we came to the school, entering the playground rather diffidently. The local children already there stared at us and we stared back, not knowing what to do. Eventually a whistle blew and they all lined up, ready to enter school. Dorothy and I stood together rather awkwardly at the end of one line, ready to march in with this group.

Suddenly the teacher with the whistle swooped on us and demanded to know who we were and what we were doing in the playground. I started to explain we were evacuees from London, but this cut no ice. 'How old are you?' was the next question. When I said I was twelve, the teacher firmly told me I could not stop there, this was a junior school and they only took children up to age eleven. I meekly said my sister was only nine, so she reluctantly agreed to admit Dorothy and marched her into school while I was shown the gate. I shall always remember Dorothy's agonised glances as she was led away without me. I waved to her from the other side of the school gate and prepared to trail back to Mrs Watson.

My welcome back at the farmhouse was no more enthusiastic. 'You can't stop here all day,' announced Mrs Watson. 'You had better play out in the fields – you have your sandwiches with you.'

Though Eva did not know it at the time, this was to be the pattern for the next two months. Rain or shine, there was no way Mrs Watson would have her in the house during the day.

I was given sandwiches in the morning and not expected to appear again until she returned with Dorothy when she had finished school. For two months I roamed around the countryside, amusing myself, helping with the potato harvest, scrumping apples and generally getting up to no good.

Mum was very cross when she found we had been packed off to school without any prior notice or preparation. She was concerned for Dorothy, who was a very shy, timid child. We all met Dorothy from school that first day and Mum saw a teacher and explained our situation. They had not been aware that any evacuees had arrived in the village and knew nothing about the rest of our contingent. They agreed to keep Dorothy until arrangements could be made to unite her with her rightful school, wherever they might be.

The weeks went by. Finally, the family were contacted and told they should never have been left in Upwell.

Our coach should have been directed on to Wisbech to join the rest of our evacuation party. They now proposed moving Dorothy and I into Wisbech, placing us in a household there, but leaving Mum and John in Upwell. Mum, of course, overruled this idea unless they moved her too. Eventually it seemed easier to allow Dorothy to remain at the village school and as there was no transport between Upwell and Wisbech, alternative arrangements were made for me.

An all-boys school had recently arrived in Upwell, taking over a large mansion to accommodate the boys. Their schooling was held within this building, which also boasted extensive grounds. I learned I was to attend this rather exclusive boys' school on a daily basis and have lessons with the boys. So, after two months of running wild with no schooling since the previous July, I duly sat in class surrounded by boys and taught by masters with not another female in sight. Though it felt rather strange at first, I soon settled in and quite enjoyed this rather unique experience. Needless to say, I received much attention and rather swanned around, basking in the limelight.

Life in Upwell raised unexpected problems:

When we left London on 1 September, we had only been allowed to take a minimum of clothing with us. My top coat was my school coat and Mum would not allow me run round the countryside in this or my school uniform, which had been an essential item to pack, or so we thought.

Dorothy was also severely limited in clothes, and as Mrs Watson only had one wash day a week – Mondays – the pair of us soon began looking very scruffy. Mum did her best to keep our clothes clean but she was hard put to launder for herself and John, the water had to be carried in from the well and then heated. She had partly won the battle of lighting the kitchen range, but the old lady constantly grumbled at all the extra coal being used and the mention of washing clothes always raised objections. As no one was at our home in London, we could not have extra clothes sent on and with the onset of colder weather in October, things became difficult.

The WVS tried to ease the plight of the evacuees and rallied round, collecting unwashed clothing for our use, plus prams and other equipment for the mothers with toddlers and babies. This was all very well but the clothes handed to Dorothy and I were mostly shabby and well worn, for nobody threw out clothes in the 1930s while there was still good wear in them – they were passed on through the family until they were no longer needed. The sizing was somewhat hit-and-miss and dressed in these garments, Dorothy and

I looked like a couple of waifs and strays from the poorest part of East London.

It was worse for Dorothy for she had to go to school clad in these cast-offs, which did nothing for her self-esteem and confidence. I was given a great long coat that flapped round my calves and half hung off my shoulders. It would have taken years before I 'grew into it' as the WRVS lady cheerfully suggested. We were expected to be grateful for these offerings but both Dorothy and I hated wearing them.

Life was very difficult for the mothers with young children trying to cope with living in a stranger's house, yet it wasn't easy for the householder either. Apart from the practical domestic difficulties, there was nothing for the mothers to do or anywhere they could go. Upwell was a small village with limited public transport to the nearest town, so the mothers were reduced to walking around the lanes, pushing their offspring in the WRVS's prams.

Mum must have walked miles during those months in Upwell. Dorothy, of course, had a structured day and was sent off to school in the morning until Mum met her in the afternoon. She hated the school and was very unhappy there. She was only just nine years of age and being very quiet and shy, found it difficult to adjust.

By the time arrangements had been made for me to attend the boys' school, I too had had enough of Upwell, becoming fed up with trying to find a barn or other shelter when it was cold and wet. I often joined Mr Watson and his son in the fields – they always made me very welcome and let me ride on the backs of the two heavy cart horses they used for ploughing. If it was wet, they gave me a potato sack to drape around my shoulders. I think Mr Watson felt sorry for me being turned out in this way but he dared not say anything. We lived a very uneasy life, Mum battling with her old lady while Dorothy and I struggled along with Mrs Watson.

Early in December, Mr Merrill arrived to spend a few days with his family. He knew all too well from his wife's letters how unsettled they were and how badly they wanted to return to London. The rent on their London home was still being paid and after he'd seen the general situation for himself, he didn't need much persuading to agree they should return home. Since the declaration of war, little had happened to suggest London was at risk and thousands of London refugees had already started to drift back. A week later, the family packed their bags and returned home.

Mum was overjoyed to have running water and an indoor flush toilet again, to say nothing of our own gas cooker. Dorothy and I had our own separate beds and could go to sleep in a room free from scuttling mice. We had never appreciated before how lucky we were to have such mundane comforts until we no longer had them. We spent a somewhat muted Christmas: Dad managed to get home on a seventy-two-hour leave pass and we had a celebration of sorts.

CHAOS

Eva and the Merrills came through the war, although they were re-evacuated on two separate occasions. Being moved from billet to billet as the war went on turned out to be a fairly common experience, however.

Moving huge numbers from city to country living had several pitfalls. Twenty-first century mobility as we know it did not exist for millions of people in the 1930s. Many evacuated inner-city families had never ventured beyond the area of the street they lived in, let alone travelled by train or car to the countryside.

For those living in the safe rural areas, the exposure to inner-city inhabitants, some of whom were impoverished and illiterate, their homes in slum-type conditions, was a huge shock. Had the war started in the way anticipated, i.e. with bombings, perhaps the rural householders might have felt more benevolent towards the strangers suddenly in their midst. As it was, the situation proved fraught, often uncomfortable for many.

Britain in 1939 was very much a class-ridden society. As had been predicted, those evacuated under the official government scheme were mostly working-class evacuees attending state schools, often from large families, so this unexpected exposure to people outside their own environment was something of a culture shock for some, though there were positives too for inner-city children unexpectedly discovering the joys of the countryside for the first time ever.

Many middle-class households taking in evacuees were horrified, for instance, at the way some of the inner-city children they took in were clothed: some were sewn into their underclothes for the winter, others had no underwear at all, nor did they have a change of clothes. Vermin-infested heads were reported too: in certain parts of Wales, half the evacuees from inner-city Liverpool were reported to have had heads crawling with lice, similarly the case with inner-Glasgow evacuees sent off to rural Scotland. There were also large numbers of complaints about children wetting the bed, a condition known as enuresis.

An article in the medical journal, *The Lancet*, confirmed this, given the amount of press attention on this topic at the time saying: 'Enuresis is proved to be one of the major menaces to the comfortable disposition of evacuated urban children.'

Consequently, in June 1940 a modest allowance of 3 shillings and sixpence was allowed for householders with enuretic evacuees.

Alan Everett was a working-class child living with his parents in a council house in Dagenham, Essex, when war broke out. He was nearly five years old.

My mother and father always seemed to be deeply engrossed in conversation. Whether this was to do with the imminent arrival of my baby brother or the onset of war, I have no idea.

My fears were soon confirmed when the gas mask arrived

simultaneously with his birth, one for me and one for him. To this day I can see him nestling in the cradle-like mask. It covered his whole body and all you could see was his pink face shining through the celluloid fascia, as we re-enacted a mock attack from the enemy.

The seriousness of the situation never dawned on me until my mother tried to convey to me that we had no alternative but to escape to the country to avoid the bombing. To tell a child of little experience must have been harder for a mother than to get the message across, and even harder for me to understand that we must part for no reason, other than we might get killed in the onslaught by an enemy that we did not know. Mum's pattern of play was to say little and coax me into thinking that if all the children were going, why shouldn't I?

It finally came home to me when standing on Waterloo station with several hundred other kids as I waved goodbye to my mother. As the train pulled out, an eerie silence descended on the train. We were alone with our thoughts and then the stifled cries of children who could hardly believe that we had been abandoned – abandoned to a foster parent who had no idea of our individual sensitivity. I clung to my mum's handkerchief, which she kindly left me, and for several days her lingering perfume was my only comfort. What hell was in store for us?

The days of steam railways were fraught with delay. It must have been a good eight hours' journey to Somerset. We were huddled together like lambs for the slaughter. The gas masks that hung around our necks on string were attached to a cardboard box that nearly decapitated us every time the engine jolted. Stop and start was the order of the day.

Our arrival in Wells, which is in fact a small country town, although the existence of the beautiful cathedral makes this sleepy community a city, was a welcome relief. We literally exploded from the train to await our fate.

We had been assigned to the Packer family, a rosy-cheeked friendly lady who drawled in her Somerset accent: 'Yoor boys come with me.'

I was coupled with another boy – a big ginger kid named Alan Bone – and our transport to Priddy (a small village) was by horse and trap. Mrs Packer wasted no time and we were soon on our way. She swung the whip and away the horse went and the trap seesawed us for six miles.

Our arrival was expected and we met Mr Packer, a stocky man with arms that looked like young oak trees sprung from his torso. I could not assess him at that stage but we retired to bed that night with great trepidation, my lower jaw quivered and I just wanted to cry out for my mother. Alan and I slept in the same bed that night and we both expressed our fears for our family back home.

The following morning, Mrs Packer called us down for breakfast and I awoke to find that Alan had peed all over me. Whether this was inherent fear of the unknown I had no idea, nevertheless someone had to tell Mrs Packer as the urine had made its way through the mattress onto the floor. She did not seem too happy when I told her.

Alan pissed the bed every night after that, and Mrs Packer decided I would sleep elsewhere. But where to go in a two-bedroom cottage? It was finally decided that the floor was the only alternative and so the floor it was to be.

Alan remained living happily with the Packers for two and a half years:

I can never recall seeing my father visit me once, such was life then. The family love was only in the mind and it's amazing how you soon forget your family and adopt new, such is the versatility of the young. Perhaps our forced absence was decided by the 7 shillings and 6 pence a week my family paid to keep me there. Where could one keep a child all found for that money? All I can say of my enforced incarceration is that they were the happiest years of my life.

The timing of the evacuation also made a difference: it took place at the end of the school summer holidays, so children had not had any supervision from their school medical service for several weeks. In addition, war's outbreak came on the heels of a long bout of unemployment. Over one million people were unemployed in 1939, another three to four million were living in poverty. Family hand-me-downs and secondhand clothing were a fact of life, as were rural homes without electric light or running water. Some children came from deprived homes where, having never seen a bath before, they were terrified to use one, believing they might be drowned.

Despite all this, the individual experiences of the 1939 evacuation varied considerably. Stories like that of Alan Everett, where urban children adjusted happily to rural life, were not unusual.

Some evacuees were housed in better living conditions, which went on to have a positive impact on their lives. Kids who had rudimentary reading skills and found themselves living in a home full of books for the first time, for instance, developed a love of reading. There was a huge positive too in being exposed to a much healthier way of life, like early bedtimes, so typical of the countryside, as well as a better, more balanced diet, i.e. fresh vegetables and fruit. Nonetheless, the emotional effect of the upheaval of separating huge numbers of mothers and children from their normal environment into a very different one would prove profound and long-lasting. Open discussion of all this by all those involved did not, however, emerge until many years later. In September 1939, there was not the luxury of time or resource to ponder these complex, often painful human issues.

At the end of the day, there was a war on.

3

THE GOODWILL OF STRANGERS

The evacuation plan was conceived under the huge threat of sudden invasion, so perhaps it is not that surprising that the listing of certain areas of the country as neutral or 'safe' zones threw up some errors of judgement.

Dagenham in Essex was such an area. Today, the London Borough of Barking and Dagenham is a local authority encompassing both areas. Back in 1939, it comprised two completely separate boroughs to the east of London. Barking, slightly closer to London, was included in the Government Evacuation Scheme. Dagenham, however, was designated for the Neutral zone. After the initial announcement that the borough would be excluded from the evacuation plan there was a huge outcry of protest from Dagenham Council, the press and angry locals.

Why had Dagenham been overlooked? How could

the borough's most vulnerable inhabitants be 'safe' in Dagenham? The area included important factories – obvious targets in air raids – including the big new Ford Motor Company plant, built in 1931 on marshland by the River Thames (in 1937, the Ford plant had produced 37,000 motor vehicles). Back then, bulk supplies of coal and steel were still delivered by water transport so the Ford plant's waterside location made it suitable for such purposes – and for transporting large numbers of people.

In June 1939, Dagenham was finally designated an official area for evacuation. Other London boroughs, including Barking, had already had more than a year to organise their evacuation plans: Dagenham had less than three months.

By the time the official permission came for Dagenham to evacuate on 27 August, it was far too late to organise buses and trains to take the evacuees to safe areas: the buses and trains were all fully booked. The sole transport option was by water, using Ford's waterside location. The General Steam Navigation Company would come to the rescue with their fleet of paddle steamers and cross-Channel ferries: they could transport the thousands of evacuees by boat from Dagenham to the safer coastal ports. The boats, however, were busy – it was peak summer season for day trips and cross-Channel work. Consequently, all the boats had to be urgently recalled to Dagenham Dock by radio.

The delay in authorising Dagenham as an evacuation area meant the hasty, last-minute arrangements for the reception areas were muddled and inefficient, to say the least. Dagenham Council officials worked non-stop to organise the paperwork for the mothers and young children who were leaving; the teachers of the Dagenham schools carried out the registration of the schoolchildren. Yet when the final rushed arrangements for the evacuees' reception and billeting at Lowestoft, Yarmouth and Felixstowe were set up (by the Ministry of Health and local reception teams), there was a serious miscalculation about how many Dagenham evacuees would actually be arriving.

Far greater numbers than anticipated turned up at the reception areas, resulting in chaos. The late decision to move the Dagenham children meant there had not been nearly enough time to arrange for billeting or transport to other areas so when the children and mothers did arrive, instead of being led to billets or foster homes, thousands of evacuees were taken for hastily organised temporary shelter to church halls, schools and even cinemas, where some wound up staying for several days until arrangements could be made to transport them out to the surrounding country areas. (It is difficult to give an exact figure of the numbers involved; while 16,894 had registered for evacuation, not all of them turned up. Many changed their minds even at the point of embarkation, yet others, who had not registered, turned up.)

At night, many of the evacuees had to sleep on straw-filled sacks, resulting in some children being infested with head lice. Only the teachers managed to save the exercise from turning into a total disaster. For several days they looked after the children, cooked meals in makeshift billets – sometimes in the open air – and helped provide hot food and drinks.

Back in Dagenham, the worried parents of unaccompanied children had no idea where their children were. Eventually Dagenham Council dispatched staff to the evacuation areas. There, they went from door to door, enquiring whether a child had been billeted there.

It was a distressing and unhappy situation. Some children only stayed a week or so, though these would eventually be re-evacuated when the Luftwaffe began to bomb London and its boroughs the following year. Other Dagenham children wound up staying with their 'aunties' and 'uncles' throughout the war, only returning home after the war had ended. In some cases, this prolonged separation had a profound effect on their rehabilitation back into their families.

THE EVACUATION FROM FORDS

Over two days, starting before dawn broke on Friday, 1 September 1939, the evacuees assembled in various schools around Dagenham. It was still dark when some started to clamber aboard the waiting ferries; some had been driven to Fords in the back of bakers' vans or laundry vans, others were packed into buses but many had to walk all the way, literally marching to the gates of the Ford Motor Company's works.

THE GOODWILL OF STRANGERS

When the first of many thousands arrived at the works gates they found them closed and locked. This was for safety reasons: the blackout was already in force and it would have been extremely dangerous to have allowed children and mothers with small babies and toddlers to wander around the busy works.

In the early morning light, the gates were eventually opened and the swarm of evacuees streamed in. By then, the men at the works had become aware of what was happening, switched off their machines and went outside to help.

Many spoke later of watching the pitiful sight of small children, clutching their tiny bundles, being led in the early morning through the vast factory. Waiting at the Ford jetties, jutting out into the River Thames, were the paddle steamers of the General Steam Navigation Company.

With the help of the Ford workers, who carried the smaller children the considerable distance from the gates to the jetty, the embarkation began. When each boat was full, it edged out into the river to make its way downstream past Tilbury, Gravesend and Southend, then out to sea, heading for the East Coast ports of Felixstowe, Lowestoft and Yarmouth.

Syd Kirby from Norwich worked at Fords as a weighbridge clerk in September 1939:

I was in charge of the Road Weighbridge that night (to the right of the factory gates) and the Rail Weighbridge (to the left of the gates). There was a small office at the end of the road weighbridge for use by the factory security man so there were two of us on duty at the gates.

I arrived for work at 11pm. I was part of the Traffic Department, which controlled the jetty, estate, railways, pig-iron field [an area of the plant where a raw industrial material called pig iron, a type of crude iron shaped like a block, was stored before being used to make steel in Ford's steel foundry] and case dumps. I was surprised to find on arrival that the gates were closed and locked. Normally, only one side is closed at night.

Syd discovered that orders had been given that no locomotives were to feed trucks containing materials onto the front of the factory. Nor were they to travel on the rail track that ran alongside Kent Avenue.

Only a handful of people knew the reason why and they were very tight-lipped about it. The blackout was on, the windows in the factory had either been blacked out or replaced with steel sheets and the night itself was pitch-black – no moon, no stars, and of course, no street lights.

In the early hours of the morning, the only people outside the front of the factory were myself and the security man. We could hear a most peculiar noise coming from the road: a murmuring, crying noise. As dawn broke, we were amazed to see the whole road packed solid with hundreds of children, some with grown-ups who were teachers, and a few mums with babies and small children. They had cases and bundles, many were crying – that was the funny noise we'd been hearing.

We had found out during the night that some of the paddle pleasure boats had arrived at the jetty and that the children were to be taken on them to the East Coast. Nobody was very happy about this as we thought the ships would be very vulnerable if there were air attacks – as far as we knew, there was to be no naval escort.

When the gates were opened, there was a surge of children, most of them wanting toilets and a drink as they'd been standing in the road for a considerable time. By now, word had reached the factory. The roar of machinery stopped, the doors burst open and hundreds of men surged out to dash over, pick up kids and their bundles and also take them and their teachers to the toilet (we had two toilets in the Rail Weighbridge and they were soon overwhelmed).

In those days, no women were allowed inside the factory. Even on rainy days, male clerks were allowed to go to the offices through the works, but the women had to walk outside and get wet. Consequently, there were no female toilets in the plant, so the girls and women were escorted to the male toilets as the men stood guard outside.

The canteen in the plant was opened up and tea was made by the gallon. In the meantime, there was a steady flow of men carrying children and their baggage to the ships on the jetty. Not only were the children crying, several of the men were crying too. Even now I have a lump in my throat when I think of it all.

Eventually the boats were loaded; they sailed some time mid-morning. They included the *Royal Eagle*, *Crested Eagle*, *Golden Eagle*, *Royal Sovereign*, *Royal Daffodil*, *Queen Charlotte* and *City of Rochester*. We all returned home late and very exhausted after walking up and down the road with children, bags, etc. My wife was very worried as I was so late, and indeed that applied to many of us men.

In the end, it was really all in vain as the expected bombing did not take place until 1940 and, by that time, many of the kids had returned home. Maybe it was just as well. I went into the Army in 1941 and, saw Yarmouth and Lowestoft after they'd been heavily bombed.

A HOLIDAY IN THE COUNTRY

Katie Owen was one of seven children from an East End family who had been rehoused in the late 1920s to a small council house in Downing Road, Dagenham, Essex. She was just weeks away from her fourth birthday when she and her family joined the throng of other Dagenham families and unaccompanied children on the jetty at Fords for the evacuation from Dagenham.

What an amazing spectacle my mum must have made with her two children under five and the rest of us. Like many working-class mums of the time my mum, Grace, was short and dumpy, no make-up (make-up is only worn by women who are no better than they should be), her hair tied back in a bun and covered by a hairnet. Even on warm, sunny days, she'd have worn her coat and hat, no matter if it was shabby, and stockings – thick tan lisle held up by a penny twisted into the top. The American GIs with their nylons and chewing gum were for the future – and to my mum's way of thinking, no self-respecting woman would have had anything to do with such things, anyway.

As for us, we already had our gas masks and little bundles of possessions clutched in our grubby hands, my bigger brothers and sisters helping to steer us toddlers. They were Grace, fourteen, Bobby, twelve, Ivy, ten, Ronnie, eight, Dolly, six, me and the baby, Teddy, two.

The family climbed on board the MV *Royal Daffodil*, first launched in January 1939. It had capacity to transport just over 2,000 passengers and once it had set off for Lowestoft, the older children had a great time racing round the boat, convinced they had spotted enemy aircraft, which were, thankfully, not in the area.

In the general mêlée, I got lost briefly but eventually they found me up with the crew 'helping to steer the boat' amid the hubbub of children, chaos, confusion and noise.

When we got to Lowestoft, we were transported to a school by coach and taxis. We were each given a cheese sandwich and an apple; we went to sleep that night on straw. The next morning, people arrived to choose who they wanted to billet in their homes. No one was going to take in a mum with seven children so we were eventually split up: Mum, Teddy and me were sent to a village in Lincolnshire called Belton after spending a bit of time at a big hostel. My older siblings were sent on to a number of different billets in Sussex, Suffolk and Wales. For about six weeks, I stayed with just Mum and baby Teddy, but just after my fourth birthday, Mum decided to return to Dagenham with Teddy. Because I was four, the authorities decided I could be evacuated without her and I was dispatched – by train – to Somerset, an intrepid tiny traveller.

And it was there, in Somerset, that my wonderful childhood 'holiday' began. War was breaking out all over the world, homes, people and countries were being devastated and destroyed, yet sheltered in those sleepy, quiet lanes of Somerset, I was about to learn to love and appreciate the countryside.

It didn't start well – my first billet was at a schoolhouse, with the schoolmarm, her very elderly mother and her daughter. I was very unhappy and frightened. The daughter, well enough into her teens to go a-courting, seemed to delight in pinching and bullying me. She would frighten me by reading stories from a large book, the cover of which showed a horrendous man with long fingernails dripping with blood, an experience which still, to this day, makes me shudder when I see long, red varnished fingernails!

However, one of Germany's bomber pilots came to my aid. Lost over the Mendip Hills while on a raid, he jettisoned his bombs; they hit the schoolhouse and we were buried under piles of rubble. After being dug out, I was taken by my hosts to see their lovely black and white dog, lying dead by the garden wall, killed by the blast. After that, I was deposited briefly at a boarding school. I remember I wasn't allowed to play out with the other children because I had wet the bed.

Only then, with the war nearly a year old, did Katie's fortunes take a turn for the better. She was billeted with a woman she called 'Auntie Ada' and her husband 'Uncle George'. They lived in a large and beautiful home in Axbridge, called 'Fairfield'. Ada was very much involved with the Women's Voluntary Service.

They had two adopted sons – I can only remember John, who was in the Royal Air Force, and I was going to marry him when I grew up. Also, for a short while, a teacher stayed at Fairfield and she taught me to knit.

Fairfield seemed enormous to me with its extensive gardens, lots of fruit trees, vegetables and flowers – orange and yellow nasturtiums growing on the walls.

The weeks that followed were days of sunshine, walking around green and shady lanes, glorious hours spent in the nearby woods playing with the local children. I never met another evacuee until my sister Dorothy, two years my senior, was billeted at Cross, a village just a short walk away from us, near Compton Bishop. Later, she came to stay at Fairfield, along with the Stokeses, a family from Bristol. I attended the local village school, infants and juniors all in one large room: the village community hall. We sang songs like: 'Hearts of oak are our ships, jolly tars are our men, We always are ready, steady boys, steady!' We also had Beetle Drives [an old party game in which, upon rolling the dice, players would draw a beetle in parts depending on the number which had been rolled] and dances to raise money for the Forces. Dolly and David Stokes soon outgrew the village school and took the bus into Cheddar for senior school.

We spent whole days walking the Mendip Hills, reached through a hedge at the bottom of 'my garden'. Tired and thirsty, we would stop and knock at isolated cottages for a drink of water, always greeted with smiling kindness by those gentle countryfolk. We filled bucket after bucket with blackberries and rosehips; these were collected from us by horse-drawn cart, earning us pocket money. Great competition grew up amongst us children to see who could earn the most, though we little-uns had small chance against the big-uns.

My best friend was called Jessica, she lived in the cottage next door. She was from a large family and I was always made welcome, [I] felt at home there. One of our favourite places was the local quarry. I knew nothing of stones, their names, their uses; we played in the caves formed by the diggings of the quarrymen. Caves where the walls glittered and glinted like diamonds in the sunlight – a magical place for two little girls to play.

THE GOODWILL OF STRANGERS

Uncle George worked in the quarry, he also drove a steamroller. It would come rolling slowly down the lanes, smoothing down the tarmac, the smell of the hot tar permeating the air; a smell to bring back memories. Sometimes I was allowed to ride high up there with him, the other children swarming around. Each evening, he would take a sandwich from his lunch tin, the cheese warm and soft, saved for me to eat as I sat cosy with him in the large kitchen, while Auntie Ada cooked dinner. What wonders for a small child from a poor London home where love and cuddles were totally unknown.

I believe Aunty Ada might have been quite important in the WVS because she often attended meetings and sometimes she visited London on WVS business. She was a large lady and could appear formidable and strict, but I only received love and kindness. For a time after I arrived, she slept with me in the cubby-hole under the stairs because I was afraid to sleep upstairs.

I remember the lovely smell of Sunday roast dinners on returning from church – cakes and treats, all such a luxury for this London waif. There was a gas stove in the kitchen, but most meals were cooked on the shiny black kitchen range which seemed to stretch down half the large kitchen. Uncle George would chop the wood to fuel the stove, which also served to warm the kitchen. A high-backed settle [a wooden bench seating three or four people] and large brass plates were displayed around the wall; this was our 'welcome home' place when we returned from school or play, where we did our homework, where we played. Just before Big Ben struck the hour for the *Nine O'Clock News*, we children chose one sweet from the sweet jar, said goodnight and went to our beds – this was the time strictly for adults listening to the atrocities of war, always shielded from us.

On Saturdays, my job was to clean the big brass plates – some so big, I needed to sit in the middle to polish. To this day, I still love my brass and enjoy cleaning it.

I remember snow – deep, white, glistening snow. Snow that so covered the lanes and fields that landmarks disappeared; snow that topped our wellies as we struggled through to school. Then the snow-plough would clear a path, another of Uncle George's jobs, leaving a covering of compressed snow which we soon turned into magnificent slides. Local men went out with the farmers and their trusty dogs, well after dark, to rescue their sheep and lambs from certain death while we enjoyed snow fights and built snowmen under brilliant star-studded skies. Deep frost, thick ice and magnificent orange sunsets.

In that other world, occupied by adults, the war raged on and slowly, but surely, the Allies were bringing it to a longed-for end. Many parents were already welcoming back their children, most of whom were thrilled to be going home, though quite a few shed tears as they left their wartime aunties and uncles. Mr Stokes was demobbed and the family all returned to Bristol; Dolly had already returned home to help my mum with the arrival of another baby. I continued attending the village school – I was one of the village children, my home remained Axbridge in Somerset. My Dagenham family was barely a memory: apart from Dolly, I had not seen nor heard from any of them since the start of the war.

Unbeknown to Katie, Auntie Ada and Uncle George had asked to adopt her. 'Auntie, on one of her London visits, had visited our house in Dagenham and she wasn't happy for me to return there but my mum refused.'

In the summer of 1946 Katie finally left Somerset: 'I told Auntie and Uncle I wouldn't go, I'd run away and come back to them – I can't have made it easy for them. But one day I was driven away in a large black car, back to Dagenham. My wonderful holiday in the country had ended.'

Katie's memory of the day she went back to her home after six years in the countryside remains strangely vivid:

It's a house – the bricks are painted white but it appears so small, so dark. A house in a long row of similar houses; across the road more houses, row on row forever. Sunlight outlines two small children peering in through the back door; grubby, untidy blonde hair, thumbs in mouth, staring wide-eyed at me. A baby sleeps in an old pram, a woman stands near by – my mother, who has had three more children while I've been away, [so she now has] five girls and five boys.

So many brothers and sisters but all strangers. Only one sister, Dolly, do I know. No one talks to me – they just stare. Later, it seems so dark in this small house with its gas lighting.

I feel my way up the stairs, following these strange people; four of us sleep in one bed and a baby in one small room.

Katie's time away was never mentioned:

Things were very hard for families like ours after the war – keeping in contact with people like Aunty Ada, miles away, was pretty low on the priority list. Sometimes Dolly and I would talk about Somerset, but in time it all became as in a dream, something that had happened to someone else.

Later, when I learned of the hard times my other siblings had experienced, I realised why they just wanted to forget about it all. So, we settled back into our family, grew up, started work, married, had children and only when people started to ask questions did we look back, remember and wonder about how we'd lived in that other world.

In August 1970, Katie was holidaying in Somerset with her husband and children: 'I asked my husband to take us to Axbridge. We found Fairfield and I asked him and my children to leave me there and call back in a couple of hours. I needed to do this on my own.'

Katie made her way to the back door. Everything she knew as a child looked exactly the same: the trees, the old shed, the vegetables, the hills, all still there. Even the horseshoe over the back door. An old man answered the door, not so tall, not so muscular, but still Uncle George.

Ushered into the big kitchen she once knew as home,

nothing had changed. The big brass plates still shone down from the wall, the big kitchen table, the settle, the dresser . . . Over a cup of tea, George explained that Auntie Ada had died a few years before: 'He was proud of how he still worked in his garden but he no longer farmed, his brother had also died. He told me he did the paper round on his bike every morning for two villages.'

Then it was time to leave: 'He didn't ask how I came there or where I would go. Perhaps, like me, he found it all quite unreal – the little girl he and his wife had wanted to adopt, now a mother with two children of her own.'

They did manage to keep in touch by letter for a while – until a letter arrived from his son John to say that George had died.

'On a frosty November day, we drove down to his funeral in the old church at Cross. I remembered many of the faces in the church but no one seemed to recognise me and I didn't feel able to speak to them. I did write to John to say I'd been at the funeral – but I never heard from him again.'

Katie still lives in Dagenham: 'I've learned to love the place, know its people and made many good friends over the years. If you ask where my home is, of course it's Dagenham, but in my heart, my home is still in the fields and lanes of Somerset.'

The first casualty of the 1939 evacuation was the huge disruption of schoolchildren's education, which deteriorated throughout the war years. The children who had been evacuated privately to stay with friends or relatives in the country fared well if they were being taught in private schools; many were able to complete their education. A number of large inner-city private schools, pupils and teachers evacuated in their entirety to safe areas, somehow managing to provide continuous education through the war years.

One such school was the prestigious Mary Datchelor Girls School, located in Camberwell, South London, financed by the Clothworkers' Company, one of the ancient London livery companies. The school was evacuated from London in September 1939, initially to Ashford in Kent.

Irene N. Watts is a German-born award-winning Canadian author and playwright. In December 1938, just seven years old, she was one of nearly 10,000 Jewish children evacuated from Germany, Austria, Czechoslovakia and Poland as part of the Kindertransport, the British-organised effort to rescue children from Nazi persecution in those countries.

On 1 September 1939, less than a year after arriving in London, Irene found herself, as a pupil at the Mary Datchelor Girls School, being re-evacuated by train from London to Kent.

I cannot recall being formally told that war had broken out. Maybe the adults thought it was like osmosis, that we just knew. Of course, my English was not yet perfect.

Perhaps I presumed 'this is war'. After all, it was like the Kindertransport: the same label around my neck, another train and people waving and crying goodbye. The days between 1 and 4 September, I spent being found a suitable billet – not easy to place a little foreigner with a German name and Jewish, many people had never met a Jew before.

After lots of knocking on doors by my teacher, I was taken in by a lovely girl, probably about ten years older than me. She was on her honeymoon, her new husband had just joined the Navy. I was there for a few weeks. On one occasion my hostess sent me to the village (Hothfield) to buy a loaf of bread.

I was thrilled to be trusted, but on the way home I lost the change in the grass. I was heartbroken, but I did not hear one cross word. Then the school opened a hostel for a dozen or so of us younger pupils in October. It was in a beautiful old farmhouse, but I was terrified of cows. I remember a man shouting 'A calf is born' and I hid because I thought he'd said there was a bomb.

In June 1940, the Mary Datchelor School was re-evacuated to Llanelli, South Wales, for the remainder of the war. Here, Irene continued her education, completed degrees in English Literature and Modern History at Cardiff University, married, had four children and subsequently emigrated with her family to Canada.

State-school pupils had their education severely disrupted by war, wherever they were. Evacuated children often had to share the premises of local schools. They were taught in shifts, attending school for half the day, the local children taught for the other half-day. Often, evacuees wound up being taught in village halls in big classes alongside children of different ages.

In the cities where children remained at home, state education was equally haphazard, with school premises frequently commandeered for civil defence purposes. During the war, many state schools were bombed.

In the first winter of war, 1939/40, many of the 200,000 children who had remained in London, or who had returned home for Christmas, did not receive any education at all. Teachers who had accompanied their pupils to the reception areas frequently followed their pupils when they returned home to the cities. Some took the initiative and offered private tuition for those families who could afford it. Others volunteered for a home-tuition scheme under which children could join classes held in private homes – or in any building that could be used temporarily.

Lilla Fox was a young teacher working in Dagenham, Essex, in 1939.

At 4am in the dark, we gathered all the children and their younger brothers and sisters at the school and then led them to the Dagenham Docks. At the docks we found two paddle steamers waiting for us – we had no idea they would be there and we had no idea where we were going. My school was girls-only, but on the boat, we had the boys' school as well. The boat was absolutely packed, it was a wonder no one went overboard. As it got light, it turned into a beautiful bright September day. Everyone was so well behaved, considering we had no idea where we were going.

Eventually we stopped at Great Yarmouth. We were taken to a school, where I was put in a metalwork room with my pupils and their siblings. In the night, we were woken by an air-raid siren and we were instructed to take all the children outside, but nothing happened. Next day, there was a huge muddle as they tried to sort out where all the children would go. My headmistress was a fierce lady but for once this worked in our favour as she was able to organise accommodation for all the children in our school in the same village – other schools had their children spread over lots of different villages.

For all the children from my school, it was their first experience of the countryside. Thatched houses, stone cottages, lots of sunflowers . . . It was a huge culture shock for the children, yet most of them behaved very well. We shared the local school – they would teach their children in the morning and we taught ours in the afternoon.

At first, us teachers were living in an upper-class hotel right on the edge of a cliff. There were still paying guests in the hotel so we had to use the back stairs and eat our meals separately. After a while a few of us moved out into a bungalow with some people who had not taken in any evacuated children.

Most of the time we enjoyed being there. The young children were fascinated by all the animals in the country, especially the pigs. But after a while children drifted back to Dagenham – it seemed safe for them to be there – so eventually we teachers were sent back too. We weren't allowed to teach at our Dagenham school as there was no [air-raid] shelter there. Instead, we set work and the children came in to collect it and do it at home. Finally, when a shelter was built at the school, the children could come back to lessons.

Eventually, it was decided it was too dangerous for the children to remain in Dagenham, so Lilla and the children were evacuated again.

This time it was much better organised and the children were sent to a village in the Cotswolds. I joined them a couple of days later because I had fallen off my bike when I was cycling in the blackout. Again, we shared a school with the local children and again, after a little while, the children drifted back home. So again, we were sent back. But this time things were very different. It was September 1940 and the Blitz had started; by then, most of the male teachers had been sent off to war. Things had really changed.

The Blitz (September 1940 to May 1941) would devastate British cities and ports, including London, Birmingham,

Belfast, Coventry, Glasgow, Liverpool, Sheffield and Manchester. Yet even before this, a second wave of voluntary evacuation took place in 1940 when 200,000 children were moved from Britain's cities to safer, rural areas.

That spring, as the German forces attacked and overran Denmark, Holland, Belgium, Norway and, eventually, France, forcing the evacuation of British and French troops from Dunkirk, the Phoney War ended. Understandably, many well-to-do families were now determined to get their children as far away from Britain as possible. Around 14,000 children were sent off to be privately evacuated to the USA and Canada, mostly to relatives or foster families, some as part of cultural exchanges. Aware of the need to help those families who could not afford to send their children overseas, a government-funded scheme, the Children's Overseas Reception Board (CORB), was set up to sponsor children's evacuation to Canada, the USA, Australia, New Zealand and South Africa. Thousands applied.

Between July and September 1940, the Children's Overseas Reception Board organised the evacuation, by sea, of over 2,500 British children escaping the threat of German invasion. It was a well-intentioned scheme but sadly, short-lived, and ended in October 1940 – German U-boats in the Atlantic had made such evacuation attempts far too dangerous.

THE DAY WAR BROKE OUT
'I WAS ONE OF THE LUCKY ONES . . .'

John Baker, seven, and his brother Bobby, twelve, were amongst a hundred children who boarded the liner SS *City of Benares* when it set sail from Liverpool to cross the Atlantic to Canada on Friday, 13 September 1940. Ten of the hundred children aboard, some travelling with their parents, were from families who had paid privately for the journey. The rest were travelling free of charge, courtesy of the government-funded CORB scheme.

The Baker family lived in Southall, West London. Milkman Albert and his wife Lucy had opted to apply for the CORB-sponsored scheme some months earlier. By the time the Baker brothers boarded the ship, the Blitz – the massive, round-the-clock air raids on London and other industrial cities – had just started.

'My mother had two sisters in Canada so as we'd be living with family, my parents decided to apply to send us,' recalled John, now eighty-five. 'I was told it was a holiday and we'd be staying with our aunt and uncle – I was very excited.'

Ten children from Southall, including the Baker brothers, were accompanied by an adult guardian as their journey began on the London to Liverpool train. (Each group of ten children on the CORB scheme had to be escorted by an adult guardian.) The passengers stopped in Liverpool for a few days.

The luxury liner *City of Benares* was four years old and had recently been commandeered into service in the

CORB scheme. This was to be its first Atlantic crossing. Finally, it set sail on 13 September. The Baker brothers were enthralled by their journey on the big liner.

'The food was wonderful. We'd been living with rationing and suddenly we could have anything we wanted, things like ice cream and peaches,' recalled John.

The brothers shared a cabin in the bowels of the ship with two other youngsters. John was always wandering off and getting lost, trying the patience of Bobby, who was looking after him. For John the big attraction was the restaurant and the ice cream so Bobby kept having to dash off to find him.

The ship's crew knew that German U-boats were lurking off the coast of Ireland. Some had already sunk several British ships. One, the U-48, had claimed eighteen Allied ships since the outbreak of war just over a year earlier, so the *City of Benares* was escorted in a nineteen-strong convoy for five days. But after 300 miles it was believed the ship was out of the danger zone and the naval escorts peeled off to protect other ships.

Just after 10pm on 18 September, John was woken by the alarm bell. He rushed around the cabin, waking the others. At first, they didn't want to get up, believing it was just a drill, but it was not a drill: the ship had been torpedoed by the U-48, which was in the area by chance. Within thirty minutes, the *City of Benares* had sunk.

The young passengers were ushered up onto the deck with all due haste. In the rush, John realised he had forgotten his life jacket. He wanted to go back to get it, but Bobby stopped him.

Somehow I ended up with a life jacket – I think it was Bobby's. We were packed, like sardines, into a lifeboat and they started to lower it. Then one of the davits [one of a pair of small cranes used to lower and retrieve lifeboats] jammed. The lifeboat tilted, shooting a lot of people into the water.

I was at the bow end and hung onto a thwart [seat]. The stern was in the water. I was somehow separated from Bobby – I didn't know where he was. So, the people who fell out were left behind. I think Bobby may have been among them.

The ship was still travelling at about 10 knots.

The crew managed to free the davit, but they couldn't release the lifeboat so they lowered a rope ladder and told us to climb back up onto the boat.

A sailor said to me: 'Don't look down, climb up as fast as you can.'

I went up like a jack rabbit and once we were on deck, they hauled the boat up and made preparations to launch it again.

Once on deck, John started searching for his brother desperately. 'But the deck was rolling and I nearly slipped overboard. Luckily, a sailor near by grabbed me and hauled me back.' Within minutes, he was ushered down again into a waiting lifeboat.

This time, the attempt was successful. He remained in the lifeboat with the other survivors until they were picked up by HMS *Hurricane*, which had travelled 200 miles to help the sinking ship. The destroyer then transported its shivering, dishevelled cargo to Glasgow, where John was reunited with his anxious waiting parents.

'I was one of the lucky ones. I don't remember how long I was in the lifeboat, but we were picked up fairly soon. But others were still in the water.'

Of the 406 passengers and crew on board the *City of Benares*, 258 had died or drowned, clinging hopelessly to wreckage and life rafts in the freezing Atlantic. There were 148 survivors. Just twenty of the one hundred children on board survived. John's brother Bobby was not among them.

'We never talked about it,' said John of his heartbroken parents' reaction to the tragic events.

> I suppose it was too painful. They had lost a son when they thought they were sending us away from danger.
>
> Bobby and I were typical of an older and younger brother. I was a nuisance but he always looked after me. I always felt I survived because he gave me his life jacket.
>
> He made the ultimate sacrifice.

Just two weeks before the *City of Benares* tragedy, another CORB-sponsored voyage from Liverpool to Canada and the US had ended when the vessel was struck by two torpedoes. The Dutch passenger ship SS *Volendam*, carrying 879 passengers, with 320 children among them, had also been torpedoed by a German U-boat. Fortunately, the passengers and crew got away in lifeboats and were rescued by other ships in the convoy, while the *Volendam* was taken under tow and eventually repaired to sail another day. All but one of those aboard survived. But after this incident, and the loss of the *City of Benares* with so many lives, a huge public outcry led to the cancellation of the CORB-sponsored evacuation scheme: it was just too dangerous.

4

THE DAY OUR LIVES CHANGED

THE BROADCAST BY PRIME MINISTER NEVILLE CHAMBERLAIN on 3 September 1939 was destined to be remembered in many different ways. These are some memories of that day:

THE TEACHER

Mary Preston* was a Liverpool school teacher, aged twenty-six. On the day war broke out, she had already arranged to help evacuate a group of schoolchildren by train from Liverpool to Shrewsbury. (Throughout this text, names marked with an asterisk have been changed.)

Nine am. Ate a normal breakfast when notice of ultimatum came through. Very upset.

Lines of 'the naked earth is warm with spring' ran

through my head. Went upstairs, read the poem 'Into Battle' by Julian Grenfell [soldier and celebrated First World War poet who died of wounds in 1915]. Got very upset about it all and had a good cry. Packed up my goods and went out at 11am, specially to avoid emotion at 11.15. Saw friend evacuating blind people. Had two hectic hours shepherding mothers and half-Chinese children to station.

Were given a corridor train which stank. When under way, two of us sat in corridor on floor, eating lunch. Nasty way of feeding but preferable to howling kids and smelly mothers. Went long way round to Shrewsbury. Had to nurse dirty baby, which smelt. Lorna [another teacher] doused it in scent to try and make it sweeter.

Reached Shrewsbury at 5.10. Met warmly but think people in billets will be amazed when they find dirty dock women to be their guests. Buses and excellent organisation by billeting officers.

Offered tea and a night's rest by a resident. Went for tea and had a good wash. The people were kind. We had a lovely tea and discussed the situation. They had a lovely view across the Severn to Wenlock Edge, Clee Wrekin and so on. We went to the station to see about a train. Evacuation train in the station. On enquiring, we found one of our staff on board and held shouted conversation with him. It was lovely seeing him again.

When the train had gone, we drank Rose's lime juice in the bar. Talked, watched the stairs and paced the platform, smoking. A troop train came in. Ours was fearfully late. We chatted with the lads and generally enjoyed ourselves for a few minutes.

Lorna and I had sandwiches, which we gave them. Then we had a fierce chase to get our train from another platform, where the three of us got a carriage with two men in it, a signalman on the railway and an Irishman from Scotland Road [in Liverpool], who had spent the day looking for his wife and children to get them reunited. An inefficient headmaster had run the party and wasted a weekend instead of collecting his party.

Then Lorna and I tried to rest, but the men talked. At Chester, the signalman got out and in came two women with four yelling children and a henpecked little man. But aggressive female plonked next to me and almost sat on me. They criticised the scheme because (a) they had no one to cook for them and (b) they had no one to mind the children. In the end, Lorna and I parked in the corridor and let the babies howl. The little Irishman joined us because he said folks had to put up and they in the carriage from the slums were just lazy sluts who let anyone drag up their kids.

It was a lovely night. There were many soldiers on our train – reporting to barracks, I suppose. At Woodside [the Birkenhead ferry terminal], we made tracks for the 11.45 ferry. Up on the top deck, the night was perfect – the shimmering river, black buildings and a few dim shapes of ships with navigation lights and the moon bathed it all in silver.

We caught trams to different parts of the blacked-out city bathed in moonlight. How I love clear, unsullied moonlight.

It made me think of my childhood before there were electric street lights in our village. I had to walk the last quarter-mile home. Then at 12.45, I reached the house and had a small supper and went to bed at 1.30. I was soon asleep after a wearying day. My clothes lay on the floor and I did not unpack my rucksack.

THE CORNET PLAYER

Ken Hone (1922–2019) was a seventeen-year-old, living with his family in Morriston, near Swansea, the eldest of four siblings. Since the age of eight, he had been playing the cornet in a local Salvation Army band every Sunday.

The band was a big part of my life. That day, we were playing at the 11–12am morning service as usual when the person in charge told us what was happening. We were all seated in a semi-circle facing the stage. We all looked across at each other, we didn't say much. I was one of the youngest there, but eventually, five of us in the band would go into the Forces.

My father was in the First World War as an eighteen-year-old. He'd come through major battles in France, just twenty-two when I was born.

At that moment, you knew your life was going to change but what would happen next was the big question. At the time, I had a good job, working as an insurance agent, but I'd always wanted to go into the RAF.

We just carried on as usual – went home to lunch, came

back to the Sunday School in the afternoon. All the young people were there as usual, but in the evening, it was packed – the town was agog that war had started. Of course, everyone went to church then. There were thirteen places of worship in our town, all of them packed that night.

All my brothers were younger than me, the youngest, aged eight, was Alan. The news didn't register with them at all. But my father had been in the trenches, he didn't have any great love for Germany in the first place. My mother wasn't a crying person – she was a Londoner, a tough nut.

We'd moved into a brand-new council house in 1927, a fantastic community, forty kids in those eighteen houses and everyone pals – a great place to be in. We had three bedrooms, a small lounge and kitchen, bathroom and toilet, a modern house. We got a radio in 1936, but no phone. There'd been a lot of unemployment in our area but just before the war, things started to buck up in the steel and tin-plate works, a lot of work for that time and a big move from unemployment. We didn't realise it at the time but the government knew more about the potential for war than we did.

At the end of that day, I just kept wondering what will happen. We had no concept of the changes ahead, but a lot of people I knew had already joined the Territorial Army – after all, it was a means of getting a few pennies. Mostly these men were in the South Wales Borderers, that was the regiment. A lot of them wound up in Dunkirk – my generation was heading for the Forces and that was it.

Sure enough, life didn't change for us straight away, no air-raid alarm – the first air raid in our area was in 1941 and the first bomb in Swansea was in February 1941 and it was blitzed for three days, 230 people killed – the bombs weren't supposed to get that far.

That day, in our house, the only person that felt badly was my dad. The chances were he could have been called up again but he wound up as a leading fireman in the Fire Brigade. The only time I ever saw him upset was in Swansea during the Blitz. He said he could not believe what had happened after what he had been through as a young man.

Two of us from the band signed up to join the Forces in 1940. I was not conscripted, I volunteered to sign up for the RAF – five minutes to join and six years to get out! I was a despatch rider for the Home Guard before I joined up, delivering messages in the middle of the night.

THE SPITFIRE WOMAN

Molly Rose (1920–2016) spent three years as a pilot for the Air Transport Auxiliary (ATA), delivering brand-new planes from factory to RAF airfield, flying thirty-six different types of aircraft, including Spitfires and Hurricanes, through the war years.

In 1939, she was an eighteen-year-old ground engineer, working in the family aviation business, Marshall's of Cambridge. Launched as a small garage in 1909 by her father, David Gregory Marshall, Marshall's expanded over time into an internationally renowned aerospace engineering company with its own airfield (now Cambridge Airport, which it still owns).

In September 1939, the threat of war was overshadowing everything. By this time, my father was spending a lot of time down at our home in Hove, Sussex. He owned a small string of horses there and that weekend, my father, my sister Brenda and I were planning to ride on the Sussex Downs on the Sunday morning. We had a Buick at the time and we had a radio. So, I drove us down to Sussex on the Friday evening and on the Sunday morning, we went up to the Downs to ride, just as planned.

We knew about the Prime Minister's announcement. And so, at 11.15am, we heard Neville Chamberlain tell the country the shocking news. We were all listening while on horseback. When the speech finished, my father said we should all ride off in different directions – he wanted to be on his own. He believed it was something we ought to take in very seriously.

I was the seventh child in a family of eight children. I remember my father saying: 'In a family as large as ours, we shan't all come through this.' So, we all rode off to meet up again in an hour.

When I thought about it, I knew he was probably right. One isn't tearful in the same way that one doesn't panic, but of course we didn't know what was going to happen. So back we went to Cambridge that same night.

By then, we were equipped with gas masks. And the sirens

went off in Cambridge the same night. We had a cellar in our house there, but we didn't go down, we just kept the gas masks with us. Which thankfully, were never used.

Showing emotion then simply wasn't done. Of course, it varied from family to family, but I think that was how people managed to get through.

THE SCHOOLGIRL

Vera Barber was a fourteen-year-old schoolgirl living in Bishop Auckland, County Durham, with her parents and older brother, Arthur.

Ours was an end-of-terrace house with a garden in front. The owner was a plumber so he had put in a bath and washbasin upstairs, but we still had to go to the backyard to use the lavatory. We were the only house in our street to have a bathroom.

That Sunday, I'd just come back from a holiday with my grandparents. They lived in Bedlington, Northumberland – a pit town. My granddad was a miner. My parents had taken me there but everyone decided I should come back so my grandparents put me on the bus and sent me home.

Of course we were expecting it. But it didn't mean anything to a fourteen-year-old. I knew my parents were feeling it. My dad, Norman, had been a soldier in France in the first war – he had never talked about it to me or Arthur. Mum didn't say much either. The radio was always on, anyway. But I remember everything going very quiet as the news sank in to Mum and Dad. Afterwards, she just carried on as usual, making our Sunday lunch of roast beef and Yorkshire pudding while I was playing around the house.

You didn't know what was to come, really. We'd been given our gas masks, tried them on – that was horrible. You had to carry it with you everywhere in its little box.

Then we sat down to eat our roast as usual – with rice pudding, we always had that.

Arthur went out on his bike – he'd eventually go into the RAF at seventeen.

Afterwards, of course, everything started to change quickly. The blackout curtains went up and children from Gateshead were evacuated to Bishop Auckland for safety because Bishop is seventeen miles inland. The school-children from Gateshead were taught at our schools so my schooldays changed. I went to my school – a county grammar – mornings only and the Gateshead children came in the afternoon. I was quite happy with that arrangement.

Not long after, we had a Gateshead evacuee living with us. Katie was the same age as me, though she wasn't with us for very long.

I left school at sixteen and went to work in a photographer's in Bishop Auckland, doing bookwork and changing plates in the darkroom. Because we were inland, we didn't have the worst of the bombing. There was only one incident as I remember it, a plane dropping its load – that was later, well into the war.

That day – 3 September – when we just carried on

as usual was really how it would continue to be for us in the war: you just got on with it. We were never hungry or anything like that; Mum baked her own bread. Ours was a way of life where you made the most of whatever you had. War didn't really change that.

THE CHURCHGOER

Christine Haig was fourteen, living with her parents in Washwood Heath, Birmingham. She had just started work in a local steelworks.

I'd just left school and my mother had already got me a job in the steelworks, so I knew I'd be going to work the day after war started. There was quite a build-up to it all during the week before, what with Poland and Hitler ignoring Chamberlain's offer – the papers were full of it.

Every Sunday, I'd go off to church: St Mark's. Our house was 300 yards down the hill from the church. The service was 10am and we knew the speech was timed for 11.15, but not everyone in our area had a radio – things were tight with a lot of people. So, we had the neighbours come in to listen to the broadcast. There were quite a few people in our house, waiting for the news: people were expecting the worst.

We lived in a rented house. I was born there and eventually I got married from there. My parents did whatever work they could; they brought in about £3 or £4 a week. We weren't poor, I'd say we just managed.

There were six houses in our terrace and six houses

opposite. Toilet and coal house outside, no bathroom, no heat in the bedrooms. Everyone said you were better off in a new council house because you got a bathroom and a toilet inside.

My mum looked after my grandmother, who lived about twenty yards away. She had a shop in the front of the house selling sweets, drapery and groceries – she'd started it when my grandfather died.

Walking home from church that Sunday morning, it all seemed so quiet, not a soul about. My dad never went to church on Sundays, but as a child, I had to go three times every Sunday. I wouldn't do that to my children, but in those days, there was no choice, you did what your parents told you. There was just the ordinary congregation for the morning service but later on, that church was chock-a-block with people.

In our house there was just my mum and dad and me, the only child, making the next-door neighbours cups of tea. My father fought in the First World War – he didn't believe for a minute that it would be all over by Christmas, as some people said.

'I know the Germans, it'll be a long war,' I remember him saying.

The country wasn't really prepared for it. The men of my father's generation knew that. My father, John Samuel James Osborne, was an inspector on the buses, but he was sixteen when he had volunteered in the Great War. He'd been in the London Royal Fusiliers – I think they took anyone, they gave him a shilling to join and he stayed until he was eighteen.

When we all heard the news, the older women started to cry. My grandma was crying. Her two sons eventually went into the Army – fortunately, they came through. I came from a military family: my uncle was a sergeant-major in the [Royal] Marines, my granddad was a cavalry. All gone before this second war started.

One or two of the women offered to help my mum wash up. The next-door neighbours just went home after the broadcast. Then we had our normal lunch. I didn't realise it, I was too young, but everyone else knew what was coming: all the talk was of rationing and gas masks. We'd already been given ours: it was horrible having to carry it with us wherever we went, though we didn't know we would never use them.

My father and two of my uncles had a little talk between themselves afterwards, discussing what they thought would happen. Their biggest worry was France, so close – that kept them talking away until about 5pm, then of course for me it was church again for evensong. So different this time, packed with people praying.

Everyone took it to heart. Usually after the church service, we had a little social club for the younger people, but hardly anyone turned up – they all went straight home. Normally we'd be playing cards and darts but not that night.

I didn't really understand it all. When I got home from church, my dad sat me down and talked to me about it. 'I don't want you to get worried, it's early days yet,' he told me. He was very good like that, my dad. But I didn't sleep easily that night. I worried: were we going to have air raids? But of course, the next day at work everyone talked about it all day long. They'd read in the papers about what had already happened in Europe. All the talk was, what would we do if they [the Germans] came over here?

THE POOR FAMILY

Jean Ledger was eleven when war broke out. Hers was a large, poverty-stricken family, hiding a scandalous secret:

I was one of eight, three boys and five girls. We lived in a small terraced house in Rochdale, sleeping two – sometimes three – to a bed. My father had deserted my mother after our youngest, Dolly, was born. He must have met someone. I was a middle child. My eldest sister Joan virtually brought us up – she helped deliver Dolly. My grandparents had three farms, so my father probably worked there.

When war broke out, I was still going to school – when my mum allowed – but my most vivid memory of the day is my brother Jack, the eldest, coming in at teatime and saying, 'There's not going to be any war' and my mother started arguing with him, 'Oh yes, there is' – the sort of thing that happens in a family.

We were poverty-stricken. We didn't have a radio, so we didn't hear the Chamberlain broadcast but we all liked reading the newspaper my mother bought every day.

We had a tough life but we didn't go hungry – my mother was a very good cook. As a family, we all lived with the shame of our secret: that our father had just walked out on all of us. Hiding that shame was very important in those days. If people knew, it was all whispers – no one ever talked to us about it.

We got National Assistance. It wasn't called that until after the war, but it was some sort of benefit which helped us after my dad deserted us. But Jack, our eldest, was a stone mason, so he contributed to the household and Jean was working too – in a factory, making shoes. My other brother Jim worked in a butcher's shop so that all helped. But it had to be hand-me-downs for clothes.

I wasn't frightened when they said there was going to be a war – I was too young to be scared, the word 'war' didn't mean anything to me. It's only when you get older that you understand the pity of it all, but on that day, I didn't understand what killing was.

For us, poverty was a way of life. My brother went into the RAF eventually, but when I look back at how we lived on so little and how we all survived well – my three children are all lawyers – maybe because we were so used to having nothing at all, it helped us get through and move on.

I went into the Land Army in my teens – hard work, but I enjoyed it. I was with country people, which was what I was used to.

THE SCHOOL-LEAVER

Just a month before war was declared, fourteen-year-old Eileen Weston left school. (At the time, the school-leaving age was fourteen; it was increased to fifteen in 1947.) Eileen was the oldest of five children.

I had dreams of going to art school but times were hard for us and the only option was to find a job. They had just finished developing the huge aircraft factory at Castle Bromwich, a few miles from where we lived in Erdington and they were advertising for staff. I wanted to work in the drawing office, they said there were no vacancies but they would be prepared to train me on the machines in the accounts section. So, I was due to start my first job on 9 September: Ten shillings a week including Saturday mornings.

I'd been reading the papers so I had a good idea what to expect, really. We knew it was in the offing. On the Sunday morning, I'd taken three of the other children to do some shopping for my mum in the old part of Birmingham called the Newton Road. Me and Raymond (twelve), Joan (ten) and Lois (four) were shopping in one of the old markets when I heard everyone talking and shouting to each other about the war.

I stopped a woman and asked her. 'Yes,' she said. 'There's going to be a war.'

I did know what it meant. My dad's brother had been killed aged twenty-four on the Somme. My grandmother knew all the stories about the first war – she'd lost a daughter to the Spanish flu [1918–20, the worst influenza pandemic in history].

My initial reaction was horror. My brothers and sisters were not as aware of things as I was – I used to read everything I could lay my hands on. Anyway, we took a bus to Aston Cross, then a tram to Erdington and all the while they were chattering away as usual, but my mind was buzzing, knowing I'd be starting at the factory in a few days' time. When we got home my grandmother, Nell, already had her gas mask on: like a lot of people, she thought it was going to start straight away. We all had the masks, everyone was told to carry them everywhere. We were just a few miles from the heart of Birmingham so a lot of the families around us were evacuating the children but my mother didn't want us to go. If the parents said, 'They're not going anywhere,' that was it. Eventually we'd go to the shelters all the time.

My fear was very real that day – fear for the family, whether the house would be bombed. In the event, it turned out we were lucky: we had a bomb outside our house that didn't explode and one bomb hit a shelter near by but there was no one in it at the time.

We remained in our home right the way through the war. And I stayed working in the factory till the war ended, though one of the factory blocks was hit in an air raid and a lot of people were killed.

Were we really prepared for war? I don't think so. I vividly remember the few cars that were on the road then already had hoods over the headlights, little things like that. And I never forgot the big drums all up Tyburn Road. The Pioneer Corps would create the smoke that came up from the drums to confuse the planes overhead. [Use of smokescreens was common in land and sea battles in both world wars.]

THE COURTING COUPLE

John Young* was eighteen and working as a counter clerk in the Post Office in Kilburn, North-West London.

For some weeks before war broke out, I had been visiting a youth club in Pond Street, Hampstead, with a couple of friends. I began to take notice of a lovely girl. In the week before war, I plucked up enough courage to speak to her. She quite happily agreed to let me walk her home afterwards – at least near to her home because on the corner of the road in which she lived in Highgate, we said goodnight. We arranged to meet again for our first date on the following Sunday morning for a walk across Hampstead Heath.

By the time Sunday arrived, the world situation had changed dramatically. Poland had been invaded, there was a threat of war and Mr Chamberlain was going to speak to the nation on the radio.

In those days the telephone was not in the widespread private use that it is now. She was not on the phone and I had no idea what her address was and therefore there was no way I could get in touch with my girl. I decided that all I could do was keep our rendezvous and hope for the best.

To my great surprise and joy she was there waiting for me. I remember thinking then that she must really like me!

Because it was such a beautiful sunny Sunday morning we decided to continue with our planned walk across the Heath. Some ten or fifteen minutes or more after 11 o'clock – when we knew Mr Chamberlain was due to speak on the radio – our happy walk was seriously interrupted by the wail of the air-raid sirens. We didn't know what he'd said but we both knew it meant we were at war with Germany.

We quite literally did not know what to do next. We sat on a bench, high on Parliament Hill, facing south towards the centre of London. We watched an RAF barrage balloon crew at the foot of the hill try, with considerable difficulty and little success, to winch up their balloon. It just seemed to flop around near the ground like a drunken sailor. We talked about what we should do for the best: should we find some shelter? Not easy in the wide, open spaces of the Heath. Should we make our totally opposite ways home to our families? Should we stay together? Without any experience of this situation we were totally confused and not a little afraid, but we agreed to stay together and face whatever was coming.

We stayed on our bench, holding hands, and gazed towards London, waiting for the skies to blacken with hundreds of German bombers coming to obliterate London and probably us with it. We hardly spoke and just occasionally squeezed hands. There were no words of undying love, we had not known each other long enough for that; there was no kissing and cuddling – you did not really do that kind of

Left and below:
The crowds outside
Number 10, Downing
Street await the
news which would
determine the fate of
the country.

Left: © Getty Images/ Popperfoto
/ Contributor
Below: © Getty Images/ Fox
Photos / Stringer

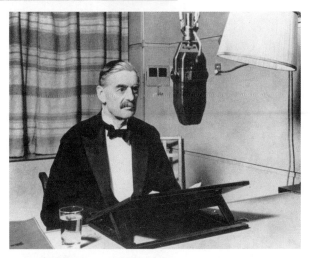

Centre: Neville
Chamberlain,
poised to broadcsat
the infamous
announcement which
was to change the
face of Britain and
the world.

© Getty Images/ Fox Photos /
Stringer

Above left: For the first time, on 3 September 1939, British citizens, some waving the cardboard cases carrying their gas masks, descend into a shelter in St James's Park, London.

Above right and below: Piles and piles of sandbags – a scene which would soon become familiar as the country prepared to defend itself from the enemy.

Preparations for war were far-reaching, requiring everyone to pull together.

Above: A group of women paint the road to guide people in the blackout.

Middle left: Gas masks were distributed – here a warden is fitting masking tape to a mask.

Below right: Rationing soon became the norm. Here is a Ministry of food ration book.

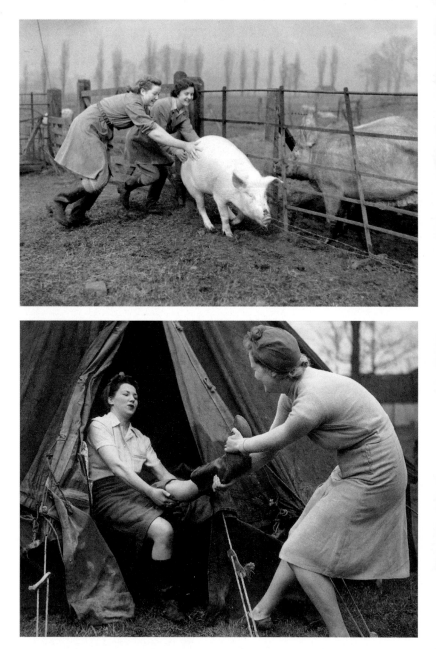

With most men away fighting, women took over what would have then been regarded as typically 'male roles' in society. Organisations like the Women's Land Army kept the country going in tough times.

Above: © Mirrorpix/ Daily Mirror

Below: © Mirrorpix/ Daily Mirror

Operation Pied Piper transformed the lives of many young children as they were transported to the relative safety of the countryside.

Whilst away many children had life-changing adventures. Inner-city children were given the chance to see outside their world of traffic and smog, instead experiencing the joys of the countryside.

The show goes on . . .

Above: A cinema reopens after temporary closure upon the declaration
of war.

Below: A group of dancers rehearse their routine equipped with both helmets
and gas masks.

The impact of the Second World War was felt throughout the country. The lives of British people – young and old, rich and poor – were seemingly altered for ever. The day the war ended was a day of jubilation and celebration up and down the country and, just like the day war was declared, would become ingrained in the memory of the nation for generations to come.

Right: Staff nurses in Liverpool celebrate VE Day.

© Mirrorpix/ Liverpool Echo/ Staff

Below: A street party in Manchester. Other events like this were happening up and down the country.

© Mirrorpix/ Kemsley

thing in public in those days. We just sat there and waited for what we thought was inevitable but nothing happened.

After a while the 'all clear' sounded and we knew we were safe, at least until the next time. We said our goodbyes and made our separate – opposite – ways home. I gave her my phone number at work and she promised to ring me in a few days. When I eventually reached home, I was instructed by my mother to take our dog Toby to the vet and have him destroyed! My parents felt we would have enough to worry about just looking after ourselves and it would be better for Toby anyway. (I never did understand that logic!) When I got to the vet's surgery, there were dozens of people with pets of all kinds apparently employing the same logic: that was a very sad moment.

Three or four days later, I had a phone call from my girl. She was now working in Central London and wanted me to meet her in Southampton Row the following afternoon. I was able to make the afternoon because I was on the early shift on the counter.

On our second date there was a surprise. She met me fully kitted out in the blue uniform of the Women's Royal Air Force: hair in a bun, flat shoes, peaked cap, etc. Apparently, on Monday, 4 September, she had volunteered for the WRAF and was now stationed at Adastral House, the RAF HQ in Theobalds Road, Holborn.

In such circumstances, my potentially great love affair was destined to fail. I could not keep in touch by phoning her although she was able to phone me at work. We exchanged a letter or two and then she was shortly posted out of London. As a result, we were never able to meet again. Our love withered on the wartime vine.

As for me, I served in the Royal Signals in Algeria, Tunisia, Sicily and Italy and was demobbed in 1946. In February 1947, I married Evelyn, my childhood sweetheart, we had three children and fifty-one wonderful years until she died in 1998.

THE TEN-YEAR-OLD

Frank Mee was a ten-year-old, living in Stockton-on-Tees, County Durham, with his parents, Charles and Gladys, and sister, Sylvia.

As a family, we went to the pictures twice a week. We watched the newsreels at each showing. So, as a lad I knew about the second Chinese–Japanese War [1937–45], with pictures of bombing and atrocities. We saw the news reports on the Spanish Civil War [1936–9]. Some local men went to fight in that and came back with stories – we knew what was coming.

My parents had seen the first war, lost relatives, seen the wounded and crippled come back. In my mother's case, she had to help two of my uncles, both badly wounded, then sent home when the hospitals could do no more. The women of the family had to dress horrendous wounds, I saw what shell splinters can do. Both uncles died: Oswald in 1921, Charles in 1933.

My mother never forgot them.

THE DAY OUR LIVES CHANGED

She had also started to lay down stores of tinned and dried food for what was to come. She also bought a lot of cloth from the market – she'd been through rationing before in the first war and knew what would be in short supply.

We lived in an area of about ten miles square, but the whole family congregated at my grandmother's house in Moses Street, North Ormesby. I've often wondered how we all came to be in one place together on that day to hear Mr Chamberlain's speech. None of us had phones, 'our' phone was the big red [public phone] box next to the pond on the Green, and the bus service was a Sunday service, yet we were all there together. And it was only at the last minute we knew there would be an announcement: was it some animal instinct that drew us all into my grandmother's house?

It was crowded. We kids went to play in the yard while the adults, looking gloomy, were sitting, talking. To us kids it was just exciting – after all, we were brought up reading Biggles, *Beau Geste*, Tarzan in the comics. What was there to be afraid of? We always won! Just before eleven o'clock, we piled into the house for the broadcast. Then we heard the Prime Minister saying we were at war with Germany.

Some of the women were crying; the men just sat there, silent. Then the air-raid siren went. I remember that moment to this day: total panic as us children were all grabbed and pushed into the large cupboard under the stairs, the very cupboard Grandma told us not to go in, because the bogeyman lived there. My sister and young cousins were all screaming in fear.

THE DAY WAR BROKE OUT

I was trying to calm my sister when the cupboard door opened and soaking-wet, cold towels were draped over all our heads – and the door slammed shut again. That set everyone off. The noise was horrendous, we could hear the adults running up and down the passage and stairs, all shouting at once. It seemed to go on forever until the door opened, we were pulled out of the cupboard and we could hear the all-clear siren.

By then my sister was hyperventilating, we were soaking wet from the towels and had no idea what had just happened. I asked my Uncle Raymond, why the wet towels? He said it was against the gas – the Germans had used gas in the First World War and were sure to use it again.

I later found out that the newspapers in the run-up to war had run the story of Guernica in Spain, how the Basque town and hundreds of civilians were wiped out in 1937 by aerial bombing by the Nazis and the Italian Fascists. The newspaper story said the Germans would open the war with a massive air attack on this country so when the sirens went off, my family thought it was going to happen, just as the papers said.

[With us] dried-off and dressed in dry clothes, Grandma and the women had, with the usual 'stiff upper lip', got the Sunday lunch cooked and served up. Granddad told us that they had been told the First War would be over by Christmas [1914] and went on for four years. Then one of the men said 'Yes, but it did not end in 1918, they were fighting into the 1920s.' 'Where?' I asked. They told me it was in the

Baltic against Russia, and in Macedonia, Iraq, Iran [then Persia] and the North-West Frontier of India. My dad, who never usually said much, said he thought it would be a long war but he hoped it would be over before I was old enough to be in it.

We made our way home and, that night, we heard King George give his speech on the radio. Mother had another cry. My sister Sylvia seemed OK by then, which was a relief as I'd thought she was going to pass out on me when we were in the cupboard. And so the day ended, one I never, ever forgot.

THE EXCHANGE STUDENT

Stella Broughton was a fifteen-year-old schoolgirl living with her family near Havant, Hampshire. Her father Charles was vice-principal of Portsmouth College of Art. In the summer of 1939, Stella was on an exchange trip to Paris with a schoolgirl friend, Maud, also on an exchange: they were scheduled to remain in Paris until early September.

During the first two weeks, we visited the Louvre Museum. Other visits were to the Tomb of Napoleon and Notre-Dame. My memory of the Sacré-Coeur is of a very long flight of steps leading up to the entrance. From there, the *arrondissement* of Montmartre appeared as an interesting collection of small, jumbled buildings nestling under the shadow of this famous church.

123

During my visit, Maud and her French exchange invited us to tea. When we arrived, we were ushered into the best room, where the table was laid with cups and saucers, a jug of milk, a sugar bowl and a plate of biscuits. Two other French girls were introduced and we all sat down. It was obviously an occasion for the teapot was brought in and ceremoniously placed in the centre of the table. The tea, when served, looked very weak but this did not bother me. What did was the fact that it was COLD! Amongst embarrassed giggles, it transpired that the tea had been made with cold water.

During my third week, there was a sense of urgency as troops began arriving by road and rail every day. The Tuileries Garden became a massive camp with tents everywhere.

Listening to the early-morning overseas radio on Thursday, 14 August, we heard someone recommending all Americans leave Europe immediately. Turning to my host, Nicole, I said: 'If it's good enough for them, Maud and I should get back to England this weekend. It appears the outbreak of war is imminent.'

By lunchtime, Maud and I agreed to leave as quickly as possible. Our tickets were checked and we were told to travel to Calais, where ferries were sailing to Dover continuously. Pooling our money, we went to the post office and sent a cablegram to my father, saying we were leaving Paris on the next midday train; would he meet us off the ferry at Dover on Saturday at about 4pm?

When arriving at the Gare du Nord, I found Maud with her French exchange girl. Her parents were quite insistent that she was to travel with us so we were bundled onto the train, luckily securing seats, and arrived at Calais about 2pm. Following the crowds to the quays, we were shepherded four-abreast into a queue, which went to and fro in an 'S' formation.

At first, we could not see the ferries or even the end of the queue for the hundreds of people with luggage. Moving slowly, snake-wise, we saw one ferry pulling away from the distant quay and within a matter of minutes, another one appeared alongside and the queue started to move again. We saw at least five ferries pull in and depart fully loaded before we got within distance of seeing one of the gangways.

'When we were within the last thirty people from the nearest gangway, off went the ferry to our left. On our right, another one was nearing the quay and yet another was steaming along, about six miles out. At last we got on board and eventually landed at Dover Harbour about 7pm.

Maud and I were through customs quickly and we waited for her French friend, who had to go through the foreign side. As she did not appear after ten minutes, I left my case with Maud and went through to the other side. No other foreigner was there and I found this thirteen-year-old girl being questioned by three customs officials. I had to explain what had happened and reassure the immigration officer that she was on a school exchange visit. After giving them the name and address of Maud's parents and accepting the fact that she might have to go back to France, I was allowed to bring her with me. Her suitcase had been taken on to London, it was several days before it arrived back at Havant.

At Dover, Stella and the girls were eventually reunited with their parents, who'd been waiting since early afternoon to drive them back to Havant. But there wasn't enough room for everyone in the car, so Maud and Stella opted to catch a train to Havant, then get a bus or walk the short distance home.

At first, Mother was very apprehensive about us going all that way by ourselves, but I said if we could arrange to travel from Paris through all the hassle of troop movements in a foreign country, we could surely manage a train from Dover to Havant. Father gave me some money and we bought our tickets.

At Havant, we were glad to see Father waiting to take us home. He'd been able to take Maud's mother and the French girl to their house. What a day!

The broadcast by the Prime Minister was expected on the following Sunday. Mother and I joined Father in the drawing room instead of going to church. At 11.15 he announced in a sombre tone that a state of war now existed between Germany and Britain. Father turned off the radio and there were a few moments of quiet thought until he turned to Mother and said: 'We must plan for twenty-five years ahead. Examination results must be downgraded immediately otherwise there will be insufficient qualified teachers available for when the war is over.'

Leaving them to discuss what needed to be done, I crept out of the room, feeling very apprehensive of what might happen and a little excited at the prospect of a very different life that might be opening up for me. My entry to the Portsmouth College of Art, where I was to spend a year, was but a few days away.

Not long after Neville Chamberlain ended his broadcast to the nation came his formal announcement of his War Cabinet. Dominated mostly by Con-servative ministers who had previously served under Chamberlain's National Government from 1937–9, one name stood out: Winston Churchill.

For a long time, Churchill's ignored warnings about Hitler had been a thorn in the side of the Prime Minister. But now he was appointed First Lord of the Admiralty, a role he had occupied in the First World War in 1914, though his part in the orchestration of the failed Dardanelles naval operation, and the disastrous military landings on Gallipoli the following year, led to huge losses and his subsequent resignation from government until 1917, when he was appointed Minister of Munitions, a post he held until 1919. Although he held various other ministerial posts until 1929, by the time war broke out he had been on the back benches for ten years.

Through the 1930s as a backbench MP, Churchill's repeated warnings in the Commons and the press about the dangers of Hitler and German rearmament had been largely ignored by the pro-appeasement government. Now, back in charge of the Royal Navy – at that time the largest and most powerful in the world – Churchill's supporters took heart: the Board of Admiralty is reputed to have sent out a signal to the entire Fleet reading, 'Winston is back'.

Yet, as 3 September drew to a close, the first major wartime blow against the British did not come, as was commonly feared, from the air. It was seaborne. And its victims were innocent men, women and children travelling to safety from Glasgow to Montreal in an unarmed passenger ship crossing the Atlantic.

The war was less than nine hours old when at, 7.30pm, the 13,500-ton passenger liner SS *Athenia*, carrying 1,103 civilian passengers and 315 crew, became the first British ship to be sunk by Germany in the Second World War, torpedoed by submarine U-30 just 250 miles north-west of the coast of Ireland. Ninety-eight passengers and nineteen crew lost their lives in the incident, which took place as the German U-boat was patrolling off the coast of Ireland. It had been at sea for several days, under orders to avoid contact or discovery.

International conventions governing submarine warfare, drawn up between the wars, stated very clearly that 'No merchant ship may be sunk without warning, and that in any case, no merchant ship is to be sunk until the safety of all passengers and crew is assured.'

The U-30 commander, Oberleutnant Fritz-Julius Lemp, had learned of the outbreak of war and had been warned to look out for armed merchant cruisers. On spotting the *Athenia*, he tracked the passenger ship for three hours before giving the order for three torpedoes to be fired.

The first struck home and exploded, ripping open the bulkhead between the engine room and the boiler room. The second torpedo misfired, and the third missed, but the damage was done and the *Athenia* started to list and began to settle by the stern. There would later be reports that the U-30 had surfaced and raked the ship with gunfire.

That first enemy torpedo had caused massive damage. In the rescue operation, one lifeboat capsized in heavy seas, causing ten deaths. Three passengers were crushed to death while attempting to transfer from lifeboats to the rescuing Royal Navy destroyers, other fatalities were due to passengers falling overboard from the *Athenia* and her lifeboats, or dying from injuries or exposure.

Twenty-eight of the dead were US citizens, leading to German fears that America would be drawn into the war.

The incident was widely reported as a war crime and the German naval authorities denied they had been involved in the sinking. At one stage it was claimed by the German propaganda machine that it had been Winston Churchill who had ordered a British submarine to sink the *Athenia* in order to provoke the US against Germany. The last thing Germany wanted was a repeat of history; it was the sinking of the British liner RMS *Lusitania* by a German U-boat in 1917, in which 128 US citizens died, that had helped bring the then neutral United States into the First World War.

THE DAY WAR BROKE OUT

The full truth of the *Athenia* tragedy did not emerge until war had ended. In January 1946, during the Allied trials for major war crimes at Nuremberg in Germany, a statement by Admiral Karl Doenitz (who signed Germany's surrender in 1945) admitted that SS *Athenia* had indeed been torpedoed by U-30 and that every effort had been made to cover this up. Lemp claimed he had mistaken the *Athenia* for an armed merchant cruiser, and at the time of the sinking took the first steps to conceal the truth by omitting to make an entry in the ship's log and swearing his crew to secrecy.

The Donaldson Line SS *Athenia*, built in Glasgow in 1923, had left Liverpool en route for Canada on the morning of 3 September, its passengers eager to escape the imminent hostilities. Among the many children on board was seven-year-old Philip C. Gunyon, born in Japan of English and Canadian parents. He was travelling to Canada with his mother, Andreana, sister Barbara, four, and brother Andrew, just two and a half. The Gunyon family had moved to England in 1938 but with the onset of war, Andreana's parents had cabled her to bring the children back to Canada.

Here is Philip's account of how the family survived the sinking of the *Athenia*:

In the early morning hours of Saturday, 2 September 1939, my mother, younger sister, brother and I left our home in London, bound for Canada. Father was in Brazil, where his company had posted him several months before. We passed through sad, quiet streets to Euston station. Silent, tired people were setting out to work, children with gas masks in cardboard boxes slung around their necks were being herded onto trains to the country. The threat of war hung over the whole country.

The station was crowded with others leaving the city for safety, mostly mothers with small children and older people. Looking out of the window as our train slowly wound its way to Liverpool, I remember looking down into the rear of depressing-looking tenements. During that trip, the only smiling face my mother saw was the agent who put us on board the tender *Skirmisher*, heading out to the *Athenia*.

She was anchored in midstream Mersey, ready for a quick getaway after loading the passengers and baggage who boarded in Liverpool. Of these, 101 were American citizens, lucky enough to have secured a berth for their return home on the last available liner.

Although very tired by now, Mother was feeling glad that we were on our way and that we children might be spared the inevitable air raids on London. But she still had a strange feeling of insecurity. Our cabin was small, with three bunks for the four of us, and she spent that first night curled up at the foot of my two-year-old brother's bunk. Other passengers settled down for a pleasant evening of dancing, card playing and singsongs.

Chief Officer B. Copeland began his usual nightly tour of the ship, paying particular attention that the blackout provisions were in proper order. Just after darkness fell, the

Athenia cleared the Chicken Rock lighthouse off the southern tip of the Isle of Man and set course on her next leg, racing through the night at fifteen knots.

The next morning, 3 September, feeling much rested, we were ready to enjoy the glorious sea air. During the day, Captain James Cook, OBE, ordered a lifeboat drill.

Athenia was equipped with twenty-six lifeboats, two of which were motorised. Capacity was 1,828 passengers. The ship also carried twenty-one Gradwell life rafts, eighteen lifebuoys and 1,600 lifejackets. Mother recalled that the officers were strict and passengers understood the seriousness of it all. Our boat station was on the deck just above our cabin. To reach it, we walked down a passage, through the smoking room, up a flight of stairs and then a short way along the deck. I recall the ship's paint, shining white in the bright sun. If the grown-ups were worried, I didn't feel that way.

Around 7pm, Mother dressed us for bed and helped us with our prayers, which ended 'keep me safe till morning light'. Putting on an evening skirt and blouse (blue with large black buttons which I loved to play with), she tucked us into our bunks with our favourite stuffed toy animals and went down to dinner.

7.39PM

Lying in my bunk in the dark cabin, I was not quite asleep. Suddenly I heard and felt a terrific thump. In later years, watching war movies which showed merchant ships being torpedoed on the Atlantic convoys, I could not reconcile those spectacular explosions with the one I had felt on the *Athenia*. Still, it was severe and the huge ship suddenly lurched and took on a decided list, then slowly went dead in the water. I sat up in the bunk and waited. I have no vivid memory of fear, only a wondering of who would come and tell us what to do next. The stewardess arrived first, followed very soon by Mother.

Down in the dining room, she had been seated at a table near the stairs. She ordered soup. While waiting for it to arrive, she read the Captain's notice apologising for the reduced level of service. The soup soon came and she laid the notice down, took up her spoon and dipped it into the soup.

It never reached her mouth. She recalled a 'tremendous thud and the crash of breaking things'. The floor seemed to lift. There were shouts and screams. Then the lights went out. She was shocked.

The stewards made for their stations without panic or hesitation. Mother made for the nearby stairs at once. The ship lurched, listed and then stabilised. She asked herself: 'Am I to die now?' Then she suddenly realised that so much depended on her. 'What will my husband feel? My children, quickly, I must reach them.'

She remembered the directions, two flights up and turn left twice. She was helped by men's lighted matches and their encouraging entreaties to keep calm. Reaching our passageway, she turned into a cabin: it was empty! Feeling desperate, she realised she had made a mistake and turned in too soon. Hurrying out, she found the right cabin and found us, 'quiet but frightened, but oh, so very brave. It was they who gave me courage.'

Together, the stewardess and Mother put lifebelts on my sister Barbara and I. Little Andrew was too small for one, so putting on a lifebelt herself, Mother lifted him up.

It was very dark and I suggested we should get the flashlight from the dresser drawer. With Andrew and Barbara in her arms and followed by the stewardess and I, we moved into the passage. It seemed smoky; it smelt of cordite. The smoking-room floor was wet and Mother fell. But she was up again quickly, and moving through the swelling crowd, we hurried to our boat station to see the boat being lowered as we arrived. The stewardess gave us two blankets and Mother gave her the flashlight as she wanted to return to see that all her passengers' cabins were empty.

Right after the explosion Mother had taken off her skirt in order to move freely.

I was wearing only pyjamas and Barbara a nightie. Andrew had on his pyjama jacket. Mother took off her blouse and wrapped it around Barbara and her stockings were put on Andrew. This left her just decent. Then she dropped one of the blankets and somebody took it away!

Now we prepared to enter our lifeboat, swinging from its davits, in and out, in and out. Someone lifted me onto the ship's rail. Looking down, I saw the dark and angry waves below. As the lifeboat swung into the rail, I was pitched headlong into it and grabbed by helping arms. How Mother made it with the two other children, I don't know. But she did.

Then began the lowering. It couldn't be quick enough for Mother. There was trouble with the ropes at one end when we finally reached the water and they could not be released. Two men who seemed to be managing things finally got them cleared, but it was a nasty moment and she dreaded a spill. I recall all of this but I had the supreme confidence of a seven-year-old that the grown-ups would eventually get us away.

We moved out quickly in case we should be drawn in by suction. A young girl took Andrew and the blanket and Mother held Barbara. I sat nearby. It was not fully dark and we could still see what we were doing. Not far away we could see the huge, beautiful ship remaining very steady and with only a very slight list.

Only later would we know that Third Officer Colin Porteous, on the bridge when the torpedo struck, had immediately pushed a button which closed all watertight doors throughout the ship. As he sounded eight short and one long blast on the ship's whistle, *Athenia* had heeled violently about five or six degrees to starboard, then slowly swung back to port and settled at about three degrees. She would remain afloat for another fifteen and a half hours and soon after 11am the next morning, tipping her bows skyward and slipping quietly, stern first, faster and faster, would be gone, her grave marked only by debris, bubbles and a vortex on the sea's surface.

Although the lifeboat was crowded, nobody panicked. There was water in the boat up to our knees and the seats were wet and cold because the lifeboat's drain plug was not in place and could not be found. People took turns bailing to keep the boat from filling up. After an hour of frantic searching, someone found the drain plug, to everyone's great relief. Although the sea was not very rough, some people were being sick. Others struck up a hymn and tried to keep spirits up by singing. That lasted for a while, but eventually everyone settled down to wait for rescue and try to keep as warm as possible.

A twelve-year-old girl gave Barbara and Mother her rug. She was wearing a warm dress and had noticed that Barbara had only a nightgown and Mother her three pieces of underwear. Towards morning, I got close to Mother and she pulled me to her. The three of us huddled under a rug like a tent, to keep off the rain and wind. What a joy it was!

We were fortunate enough to have an American sea captain in our boat and he took charge and did it well. People took turns with the rowing through the night, including *Athenia*'s nurse, a steward and an elderly American gentleman who had been at Mother's table. Towards morning, the rowers became weary and our boat began taking the waves broadside. By now, they had grown quite big. Mother had a horror that the boat would capsize. The rescue ships, *Knute Nelson*, *City of Flint* and Axel Wenner-Gren's private yacht *Southern Cross* had arrived during the night but we were far from them. [Wenner-Gren was a Swedish industrialist and, at that time, one of the richest people in the world; the yacht had once been owned by Howard Hughes.] But then, as dawn brightened, we saw two British destroyers approaching. What a joyful sight! Mother said that it was almost funny the way people tried not to sound too eager but couldn't help showing their feelings.

One of the destroyers, HMS *Electra*, soon drew near to our lifeboat. We heard words of warning, 'Sit still', 'Keep your heads', 'Just be patient', then we were alongside. Down came a rope ladder followed immediately by a great, tall, sturdy sailor. One look at him was enough – we were safe!

More sailors dropped into the lifeboat and began to get us aboard. Children first, we were boosted up and had to jump for the rope ladder as the boat came up on a swell. At this point Mother got her only injury, a bruised leg, when she swung onto the ladder and just escaped catching it between the lifeboat and the destroyer. Her only recollection of the ascent was 'Thank goodness I was once a gymnastics teacher!'

As her bare feet came into contact with *Electra*'s solid deck, she knew that all four of us were safe.

The sailors took us below and brought tea and dry blankets. Their complete understanding and wonderful kindness released bottled-up feelings and tears of gratefulness and relief came to Mother. We were all separated coming aboard and I was taken over by the torpedomen's mess. Slung up in a hammock just under a beam, I fell asleep in the warmth, crying for my drowned stuffed animals. I don't remember how long I slept, but when I woke and sat up suddenly I hit my head hard on the steel deck overhead! Lying in my hammock and feeling quite seasick, I asked where my mother was. The torpedomen soon found her and reunited us. While we waited, one of them gave me an old Leading Torpedoman's arm badge – I still have it today.

Mother had already found Andrew and Barbara and we were all taken to the engine room, washed up in buckets and changed into sailors' warm, dry clothing.

We ate too. I ate so many chocolate bars that I got sick (I wasn't able to eat them again until the war was nearly over). But afterwards we were taken on deck and the clean, fresh air cleared my head and I felt good once more.

Electra and her sister ships remained on the spot until evening, looking for the sub and watching for survivors. Towards evening, our sailor friend set out three mattresses for us on deck and settled his own on the outside. Despite a call for 'Action Stations' and a warning not to mind any depth-charge explosions we might hear, we all slept.

By the morning of 5 September, we came into sight of Scotland. How destroyers can move! As *Electra* moored, people from our mess hurried on deck, but we waited below. As our turn came to disembark, one of the torpedomen, Jack Phelan, approached Mother and pressed something into her hand, saying, 'Please take this. The men of my mess have collected it for you and the children, knowing you are without money or clothes.'

This gesture meant a lot to her and she could not reply,

holding back tears, her throat hurting and eyes burning until he was gone. Perhaps he misunderstood her silence for that December, safely in Canada, we received a Christmas card signed by the men of *Electra*'s torpedomen's mess. With it came a letter from Jack Phelan dated 23 December 1939.

Dear Mrs Gunyon,

I was very pleased to know that you and the children arrived home quite safe and going by the snaps, the children look in wonderful health. But I think you still have a lot to forget. But all that will pass in time. I have always admired your courage and devotion which you gave to your children during that time and I wanted to help to lift that burden off your mind during your short stay with us.

I have often wondered, you had my address. But you never wrote to me and I was thinking if it was on account of me collecting that small donation for you and the children, that it made you feel embarrassed to me.

Well, this is only a short note also hoping that you and the children spent an enjoyable Christmas.

Yours most sincerely,
JACK PHELAN

Once ashore, we were overwhelmed with kindness. Clothing had been collected and was handed out to everyone. Mother remarked that at some other time it might have been funny to see some people's eagerness to claim the lovely silk underwear and stockings!

Next came the trip to Glasgow by bus, a crowded hotel,

a hasty meal, everyone bewildered, loudspeakers never ceasing their inquiries for somebody or other.

At last our names were called and a friend of my father appeared like a fairy godfather. He had us installed in no time at a quiet hotel, where we rested and got warm.

Within forty-eight hours of the sinking, in Brazil my father had received three telegrams assuring him that we were safe. We spent a couple of weeks at a friend's lovely home on the moors at Dawlish in Devonshire.

I got a new stuffed toy, a Scottie dog I named Larry, to replace those that had gone down on the *Athenia*. But I still grieved mightily for them.

On Sunday, 1 October, we embarked for New York aboard the United States Lines' *Washington*, anchoring the next day off the French town of Le Verdon, near Bordeaux. Here, she debarked French passengers and picked up a cargo of wines, automobiles and other cargo. On 5 October, we left France and that is when I learned about the Bay of Biscay. We tossed, jumped, bumped and went through agony and I was very seasick. I recall sucking lemons as a cure – it seemed to work.

Arriving in New York Harbour on 12 October, shipyard workers repainted the huge American flag on each side of *Washington*'s hull, advertising her neutral status.

My brother Andrew's underpants, hung out the porthole to dry, received a coat of red paint.

That evening, we landed and drove through the darkening streets of the city to my Uncle Mario's home on Staten

Island. The next day, we took a train north and finally arrived at my grandmother's home in Oakville, Ontario.

I still have my mother's replacement passport, issued on 28 September 1939. It records our arrival in Canada at Fort Erie North on 13 October 1939. Another stamp testifies to us having been granted status as Canadian landed immigrants on 21 January 1942.

Phil Gunyon settled in Canada. Following a long career with Alcan Aluminium Ltd, he has maintained a lifelong interest in military history.

5

HOW WE LIVED THEN

On 29 September 1939, 65,000 people (described by the somewhat unlovely term as 'enumerators') were sent out to every home in the United Kingdom to register the details of everyone living in every household. This was Registration Day, planned by the General Registry Office in December 1938, and the information recorded that day is known as the 1939 Register.

In a sense, the 1939 Register proved to be a mini census of the UK population at that time. A census is normally taken every ten years. But with war fast looming, the decision was taken to create the 1939 Register as a means of recording everyone in the country who would require an identity card.

The next census was not due until 1941; it was half hoped, in 1938, that there might still be a peacetime census, making the 1939 Register an interim resource. Events, of course, proved otherwise, for the war lasted long after 1941 (a new census was not taken until 1951). As a result, the 1939 Register documents the basic details of the lives of forty-one million people as war broke out.

On Registration Day, householders were asked to complete a form giving details of everyone living in their house. In return, they would receive an identity card and a ration book in the post. Everyone needed to give their full name, address, sex, date of birth, marital status, occupation and/or details of whether they were a member of the armed forces or reserves.

The enumerator's job, going from household to household, was not an enviable one, as described in January 1939 by the General Register Office.

The qualities desirable in an enumerator have sometimes been underrated. His duties require an ability to master somewhat detailed official instructions and forms and a sufficient standard of clerical efficiency to enable him to carry out the procedure with precision and punctuality. Tact and courtesy are necessary in interviewing households in explaining what has to be done and in coping with occasional unobligingness.

A regular and clearly legible handwriting is also necessary. The element of handwriting is of importance, since under somewhat disadvantageous conditions of house-to-house visits, the enumerator is required to make entries in the schedules delivered in his enumeration book and in other documents which will serve as a basis for much of the subsequent operations.

There's no official record of the level of 'unobligingness' the enumerators encountered in their painstaking trek from door to door – you need only use your imagination. Yet the 1939 Register is, effectively, a mini-snapshot of Britain at that precise point in time and reveals, in the small detail, much about the population as it went to war.

On average, three people lived in each home. Their work or occupation gives important clues to their everyday lives; the 1939 Register shows very clearly that women at that time were still chained fast to domesticity. This would change, of course, through the war, as both voluntary and paid work for women increased. And slowly, but surely, the more affluent households were already beginning to buy labour-saving devices like the vacuum cleaner, which first became available in the 1930s. Yet the Register is still a reminder of how wartime altered the landscape for so many women. For good.

Of the twenty-two million women on the 1939 Register, nine million recorded their occupation as 'unpaid domestic duties'.

Over three million women stated their occupation as 'paid domestic duties'.

In other words, nearly half the women in the country were involved in carrying out domestic work, most of it unpaid.

The majority of the nineteen million men recorded in the Register were either retired or working in administrative work, i.e. clerical jobs. A nation of women still tied to hearth and home and men dependent on a desk job wage until – or if – they volunteered for or were summoned to enrol for military service.

Yet while the Register, now available online for England and Wales, gives everyone an important glimpse of the past, it cannot answer other big questions about the era: how were people living then? What were their homes like? How did they spend their leisure time? How did they get around? What were the elements that made up their day-to-day lives just before war changed everything?

The memories of the Chamberlain broadcast of the previous chapter give a hint of what everyday life was like for some. But a closer look at Britain in the 1930s is required.

A HOME OF YOUR OWN

The 1930s in Britain tends to be mostly regarded as an era dominated by dole queues, hunger marches, unemployment and widespread poverty. This was the time of the Great Depression, the severe worldwide economic downturn which spread across the globe after the stock market crash of Wall Street in 1929, lasting for the better part of a decade.

Britain's wealth had once come from the industrial areas of the country, the heavy industry producing coal, iron, steel, ships and textiles in the nineteenth century. Since the First World War, these older industries were undergoing serious decline. They had not been able to modernise and were badly affected by competition from other countries. As a consequence, whole swaths of the country – especially areas in the North-East, North-West, the Scottish Lowlands and the mining villages of South Wales – faced record unemployment levels. Pits were closed. Mills were shut down. Millions were on the breadline.

Unemployment benefits were minimal. They were cut off after six months out of work and the rules, even for minimal payments, were harsh and unforgiving: any woman refusing an offer to work in domestic service, for instance, would usually be denied benefits.

A Household Means Test for the dole was introduced in 1931. In many cases, the test meant officials would visit families to ascertain how much was being earned – or even what possessions there were in the home that could be sold, i.e. a piano, before a family became eligible for a dole payment. This, of course, was the cause of much anguish for struggling, out-of-work families. Any household where someone had some sort of work, such as an older child, or even a situation where a grandparent lived in the home rent-free, would be unlikely to receive any dole.

The system seemed cruel and uncaring to many. It was best described in 1931 by the writer, poet and journalist G. K. Chesterton: 'For the first time in living memory, the Government and the nation has set out on a definite deliberate campaign to make the poor poorer.' In any event, the dole payment itself – 21 shillings in 1931 for a family of five – was not enough to cover basic costs like food and clothing.

To this day, we still talk about Britain's North–South divide. Back then, this best describes the country – in much starker terms. Life in a family where the breadwinner had previously been an unskilled worker in declining heavy industry was very tough indeed. Poverty had become endemic.

Through the 1930s, there were several hunger marches to London from protesting unemployed groups of men from different parts of the country to little effect. Awareness of this huge division of society peaked with the Jarrow Crusade of 1936 when unemployed workers marched to London to petition the government. (Jarrow had been ravaged by unemployment and became an unemployment blackspot when shipyard closures left 10,000 men out of work in 1934.) Despite hugely sympathetic press coverage, however, the marchers' petition fell on deaf ears, although in the long term it would bring awareness and a change in government attitude to welfare.

Conversely, by the mid- to late 1930s, families who were working and living in the southern part of the country – the Midlands, the Home Counties and other parts of the South – were experiencing a steady improvement in their living standards. Effectively, there were two Britains in the 1930s.

In the more fortunate part of the country, new light industries had emerged, powered by electricity rather than coal, so they did not need to be built near coalfields and new factories or plants were being built closer to areas of high population, like the Midlands and the South-East.

New industries, like the car industry, brought jobs and as a result of this development of light industry, an ever-growing volume of new, mass-produced household goods, made in modern factories, advertised heavily through the newspapers and magazines of the time, were bringing small but significant beginnings of more affluence for the working population, with increasing numbers of hire-purchase schemes (an early form of credit, repaid with interest over a fixed period) also becoming readily available. Prices too had fallen during the Depression years – family sizes had also started to drop. The very first family-planning clinic for married women, offering free advice on contraception, was opened by Marie Stopes in London in 1921. Stopes (1880–1958) was an author and campaigner for women's rights whose controversial sex manual, *Married Life*, had scandalised society when it was first published in 1918, bringing the topic of birth control into public awareness for the first time. That first-ever family planning clinic in London, run by midwives and visiting doctors, moved to Central London a few years later and, in time, developed into a chain of non-governmental organisation birth control clinics across the world.

Cars, previously the sole province of the wealthy or upper middle classes, were beginning to be slightly more affordable. *The Highway Code* first appeared in 1931; driving tests became compulsory in 1934.

Two million cars were sold in 1938 and the most popular, the Austin 7 Tourer, could be purchased for £125. Given that the average wage in that year was £139 – less than £3 a week – buying a car was now within the reach of the comfortably-off lower middle classes too. Yet if cars were still mostly unaffordable, the new, tempting items that were being made in the modern factories were starting to make a gradual impact.

Locally manufactured radiograms [a combined radio and record player, usually housed in a wooden cabinet], radios, vacuum cleaners, washing machines, electric cookers and other 'modern' home appliances began to appear in middle-class homes in towns and cities that now had mains electricity. For the first time in history, a big change in women's lives was on the horizon through these new labour-saving devices.

Paid holidays for workers were introduced too – also for the first time ever. The Holidays with Pay Act of 1938 introduced one week's paid holiday a year for all working-class employees. (Until then, only around four million manual workers were entitled to a holiday with pay.)

Younger, unmarried, working-class women, for whom the only route to employment had been domestic service and little else, were discovering less back-breaking, albeit low-paid work in shops and offices in the fast-growing larger towns or cities.

Public transport also developed rapidly in the 1930s, with increasing numbers of trolley buses (electric buses that took their power from overhead cables via two trolley poles on the vehicle's roof), electric trams and trains moving people from workplace to home, especially in London, where the Underground was expanding as never before to link homes in the fast-growing outer suburbs directly to Central London, all broadening working people's horizons.

Glamour also made a huge impact. This was a time when the powerful influence of Hollywood ensured that the movies became the most popular form of entertainment. By 1938, there were nearly 5,000 cinemas in the UK, some of them hugely exotic architectural works of art, seating thousands.

People flocked in droves to the cinemas that had sprung up in cities and towns from the late 1920s onwards. The high-octane allure of movie stars like the glamorous Jean Harlow, the enigmatic Greta Garbo or the urbane Cary Grant projected a compellingly enticing vision of a world of luxury, romance and sophistication – a fantastic escape from reality for the price of a ten-penny ticket to the flicks.

THE HOUSING REVOLUTION

Underlying the huge contrasts of the era and the North–South divide is another, slightly less-heralded, story of growing living standards – led primarily by the late-thirties changes to the housing landscape.

By 1938, when much of the worldwide economic recession had ended, there was a house-building boom in Britain. Suburbia, as we know it today, expanded greatly at around this time, helped by improved train services, while a new and much-needed approach to house-building had started with the introduction of local authority-subsidised council housing.

After 1933, the worst of the nineteenth-century slums of Britain's inner cities, dark, vermin-infested, insanitary rented homes not fit for habitation, were beginning to be demolished by local authorities. Unfortunately, the task was only half-complete by the time war was declared (though in one way, it could be said that Hitler's Luftwaffe carried out some of the other necessary demolition work).

In fact, by the time the Second World War began, more than four million new homes had been built in Britain in the 'between-wars' period. By 1938, three and a quarter million people owned their own home or were buying one with a mortgage of repayments usually spread over twenty-five to thirty years.

A lower middle-class couple, with the white-collar worker husband earning a respectable £200 a year (just under £4 a week), could buy a semi-detached house in a suburb of London for under £600 with a mortgage from a building society, repayments sometimes costing just £1 a week. Row after row after row of these new, bright homes sprang up on green fields outside the cities and along the coast. Brand-new crescents, drives and avenues began to take over the areas outside urban centres.

Ninety per cent of these homes were built for sale on suburban estates by private builders; one million brand-new council houses and flats for rent were built by government-funded local authorities, replacing some of the worst slums.

By 1939, nearly a third of the population were living in post First World War houses. And home ownership, which had made up just under 10 per cent of all housing in Britain before 1914, rose to 27 per cent of all British homes by 1939. The elite disliked the new suburban houses, however. Given that class distinctions were still so dominant in the pre-war era, there was a lot of snobbery about the new homes. But millions moved in – and loved them.

Those who aspired to buying a new home, mostly lower middle-class working families, were often couples or families who had previously rented in crowded inner-city areas. The opportunity to have their own brand-new home, front gate and door, plus garden, front and back, was virtually a dream come true.

Mortgages for housing via a building society loan had only been available to the very wealthy in previous times so this was the first time ever the funds to buy a home on a mortgage became more widely available. Being an owner-occupier was a major step upwards.

Renting a home, while still the only option for the

majority of families, was a fairly straightforward process in the 1930s, as was moving house, as Eva Merrill recalled.

> Father always managed to find work, not easy in the 1920s and 1930s, but he was very adept at turning his hand to most things and had a good work record. Moving house was also very easy. Houses and rooms to let were advertised in every area and it was a matter of days to pick up one's bits and pieces and move house to another location. One week's rent in advance was all that was required and one week's notice to the current landlord.
>
> I can remember going with Mother in the 1930s, looking at numerous empty houses and rooms. She'd say, 'Let's go and look at some houses' and off we'd go, collect the keys from the estate agents and look around. She had no intention of moving, she just liked viewing different houses and seeing what was on offer, much as one goes window shopping.
>
> Of course, if the rent wasn't paid on the dot, you were likely to find yourself and your possessions dumped on the streets; no going to court for a possession order, or the like, quick, rough justice all round. No rent, no home.

This harsh practice also applied to families who were moved by local authorities from slum or sub-standard dwellings, due for demolition, into newly built homes.

Another aspect of the quiet housing revolution was that the one million brand-new council homes for rent were built by local authorities to high standards hitherto unknown to working-class families. It was recommended that the standard of building should allow such houses to last for at least sixty years, with a minimum of three bedrooms – living room, parlour, kitchen and scullery on the ground floor and three rooms on the floor above. There were indoor lavatories, bathrooms, a larder, hot-water supply and gardens rather than yards. For many families this was a near-miraculous transformation.

'Because we had no indoor lavatory, the use of chamber pots was part of our everyday life,' wrote author, poet and philosopher Bryan Magee of his childhood in 1930s Hoxton, at the time one of London's worst inner-city slum areas. 'There were always two pots under each bed upstairs. And they were called "the po". I was supposed to try hard not to use the po and use it only when I had to.'

RAF veteran Ken Hone recalled vividly the time he and his family were moved into a brand-new council house for rent on a small housing estate in Morriston, near Swansea, in 1927.

Just five years old, Ken was awestruck by their new surroundings, the three separate bedrooms, a gleaming bathroom and toilet upstairs. To such an extent that the first time he used the brand-new toilet in their home, he pulled the chain to flush and upon hearing the noise, ran, terrified, down the stairs to the living room.

'It made a noise I'd never heard before,' said Ken. 'To us, coming from very cramped conditions indeed, the new house was a palace – there was no other word for it.'

While the late-thirties housing boom would not yet eradicate sub-standard or slum housing, it did mark the beginning of an improvement. By 1939, 245,000 slum houses had been demolished or boarded up – though close to half a million slum dwellings remained in cities and towns.

BRIGHTON'S SLUM CLEARANCE

Inner-city Brighton had some very bad slum housing dating back to the early 1800s. In 1921, the popular seaside town was the second most-populated county borough in the country, an area with an urgent need to house its working-class population in better accommodation.

Through the inter-war period, Brighton demolished 900 slum homes and built 4,285 brand-new council homes in areas just a few miles to the east of the city centre, much of which had previously been open farmland.

The new council housing extended up the Bevendean Valley to form the Bevendean Estate: land was purchased by the council in 1935 to create the East Moulsecoomb Estate and, the following year, work started on building homes on the Manor Farm Estate.

As a social experiment, Brighton's 1930s slum clearance was only partially successful: the rents on many of the newly built estates were often too expensive for those being rehoused.

A new two-bedroom house on the East Moulsecoomb Estate, for instance, could be rented for 12 shillings 7½d;

slum-clearance families were even given a 25 per cent rebate. But when you consider that in an unemployed household, a weekly dole payment could be just £1, quite often the choice between feeding a family of three or four children and paying the rent meant that food usually came first.

Brighton's slum poverty, however, bad as it was, was not quite as extreme as it was in some of the industrial inner-city slums simply because as a seaside town, there was always some food around, for instance free fish scraps from the beach or from the many smokeries in the area. But too many Victorian-era small houses crammed close together, with inadequate sanitation, overcrowding and poor water supply, meant nonetheless that inner-city life in Brighton's back streets was, to twenty-first-century eyes, a shocking state of affairs.

FROM A SLUM TO A PALACE

Preece's Buildings, built in the 1820s, was a tiny cramped cul-de-sac between Gardner Street and Regent Street in central Brighton. The Buildings were demolished by the local authority in the late 1930s. Today, the area forms part of the much-visited fashionable North Laine district.

Victor Cox grew up in Preece's Buildings in the twenties and thirties.

My parents got the house on the condition they decorated it, for a rent of 5 shillings a week. I was the first child in the family to be born in a house. My father was a horse trader but he became a labourer and scaffolder and took what work he could get. My mother went out cleaning in a house in Powis Square and in two pubs.

Our house had three floors, was cobbled outside and had only one small room on each floor, about eight feet by nine feet square. The top room was even smaller as it had a sloping roof. As you came in, the stairs were straight in front of you. The downstairs room was the only room to live and cook in. My mother cooked on the fire and the black grate by the side of the fire.

We had no back door and no yard as our house joined the cork factory which supplied a cork shop in Gardner Street. We would lie awake at night and hear the machinery going. There was only one way in and out of the house, through the front door. My mother lived until she was ninety-seven. She often said we could have been burnt alive.

We didn't have much furniture in the downstairs room, only a table and kitchen chairs. There was just room to pull the chairs out and sit down at the table, so you can see how small it was. When the coalman came to put the coal under the stairs, he had to open the door to this room and we had to move the table over to make space. On the first floor was my parents' bedroom, but you couldn't light a fire there because it would have set the bed alight, it was so close.

To reach the top floor, you had to mount a curved staircase where we children slept in two beds, 'top and tailed' [two people sleeping with their heads at opposite ends of the bed]. The room was very cold. We never had a light even when gas mantles were put in the other rooms and we continued to go to bed by candle light until we left the house in 1936. Until 1927, the only lights in the house were oil lamps and candles.

As there was no backyard, we had no running water. You had to go out of the house just to get a glass of water. Each house had its own WC, but we had to share the wash house, used in a rota system by the women. When the clothes were clean, they were rinsed and put on one of the lines across the street. When we came home from school, we had to dodge in and out of the washing to get to our front doors. If it was wet, the washing would be draped over lines inside the house, which was not pleasant.

Everyone helped each other in those days. It was a hand-to-mouth existence but everyone was the same. Sometimes the rent money was late and I would have the job of taking it round to the landlord. If kids were ill, the neighbours would rally round to help.

In 1936, the family learned they were to be rehoused: the Buildings had been scheduled for demolition.

Manor Farm was the area we were to be moved to and I went with my father to look at the estate. The houses were like Buckingham Palace compared with Preece's Buildings, having running water, a bathroom, plenty of living and sleeping space and electric light with just a switch.

They also came with an electric cooker with the Corporation crest on it and an electric kettle. My mother was always afraid of electricity, she didn't want to use them.

THE BLACK SPOT OF BRIGHTON

Oxford Court was a side turning on the south side of Oxford Street, near London Road, Brighton. Built in the mid-1820s and demolished in the late 1930s, such was the Court's reputation that it was known locally as 'The Black Spot of Brighton', a poverty-stricken street surrounded by pubs.

From the *Brighton and Hove Herald* dated 24 March 1928:

FAMILY IN A CONDEMNED HOUSE

A Scandal to Brighton

Sensational disclosures of the conditions in which a family of six have been living in a condemned house in Oxford Court off Oxford Street were made at an inquest at the Brighton Town Hall on Thursday.

The Borough Coroner was inquiring into the death from laryngitis and measles of a child aged three years and seven months. She was Irene Esme, the daughter of Arthur Cecil Leighton, a furniture porter, of 3 Oxford Court, who is now out of work and in receipt of a 'dole' of £1.

The Coroner said: 'I have visited a good many poor homes but I must say I have never visited a place as terrible as this house. It is extraordinary that a town like Brighton should have three cottages without any sanitation except an open closet and there should be no water. The property ought to be pulled down, there is no question of that. I don't know who the landlord is, but I don't think he ought to take rent for them.'

Leighton said that he paid 6 shillings a week rent for two rooms, one upstairs and one down. There was no closet in the house. There was a closet attached to a house three doors away; this closet has a water tap outside. Three houses have to use this closet and the public can use it as well as there is no door to it. He added that the house was condemned two years ago but he had been unable to obtain other accommodation. The bedroom used by the family measures 12 feet long, 8 feet wide, 7 feet high.

Replying to the Coroner, Leighton said that a nurse from the Health Department had expressed herself satisfied with the condition of the children. There was nothing wrong with the children until about a week ago. The eldest girl then showed a few spots on her face and was sent home from school because she had a cold. He did not send for the doctor. On Saturday last he found that the other three children had colds. They were kept in bed, given extra nourishment and rubbed with oil.

On the following Saturday he noticed that the girl Irene was not so well and had difficulty breathing. On Monday she was worse and a doctor was sent for. Dr Fraser, who was called, said he should inform the health authorities. Later the Medical Officer of Health arrived but the child was then dead. The other children were sent to the sanatorium.

The Medical Officer said that when he was called to the house he saw that it was in a deplorable state.

'I went upstairs and found three children lying in the bed. They were obviously ill. The eldest of the three was desperately ill and dying. I was of the opinion that she was suffering from laryngitis and measles.

'Between two and three o'clock in the afternoon I found the child lying dead beside the youngest child and the second child appeared to be worse.'

The brand-new local authority housing built in London in the 1930s was not entirely the result of slum clearance – only a small proportion of the new housing came under that category. The then London County Council (LCC) built over 89,000 new homes in the years between the wars.

In 1924, the LCC decided to establish a number of new housing estates for working-class families in what were previously rural areas outside London. Known as 'cottage estates', these were planned to provide housing 'fit for heroes' in the wake of the First World War. One of them, the Watling Estate, in London's Burnt Oak area, was designed to provide new homes for families from inner London areas. It was finally completed by the mid-1930s.

At the time the Watling Estate was completed, however, there was little other than the new housing, with few shops or facilities, making it a difficult option for families accustomed to all the conveniences and shops of the inner London areas. Many new residents, despite the opportunity to live in a green areas in vastly better housing, did not stay on the estate. Additionally, the 'snobbocracy' – as the local paper described the residents in surrounding areas – did not relish a working-class estate in the area. As with the new council estates outside Brighton, too, many families found they could not pay the rent and were subsequently evicted. Rents on the estate varied from less than 4 shillings 2d for a two-room flat £1 3 shillings 8d for a five-room home – almost double the inner-city rents previously paid.

By the end of the 1930s, however, the Watling Estate's population was 19,000, nearly half of whom were under eighteen, living in households where most breadwinners worked in skilled or semi-skilled labour, transport or clerical work. In 1937, half of the men on the estate were earning between £3 and £4 a week.

'IS THIS ALL OURS?'

May Millbank lived on the Watling Estate in the 1930s:

I was seven when we moved from King's Cross to Watling, that was back in May 1937. I had never been to the country before and so I had no idea what it would be like. We were told the house was situated near a park and Father said there was plenty of grass. I would dream about parks with grass and roundabouts and swings. I'd seen grass in picture books, but I didn't know what it really was so I had to imagine.

We moved to Watling in an old coal van – my father had to help the coalman do some deliveries to get the money for it. It was pouring with rain the day we moved. Mum was in the front of the lorry and the furniture, along with us kids and Dad, was in the back, under a tarpaulin. The journey was about an hour and we was like wet rats when we arrived.

As we were brought into the house we thought, 'Is this all ours?'

I remember saying to my father, 'Where are all the other people?'

We looked out of a window and my brother, two years younger than me, said: 'What's that over there?' He couldn't make out what the green was or what the flowers in the garden were and I was glad he asked because I wasn't sure if the flowers were also called 'grass'.

Pat Cryer grew up in a typical 1930s semi in Edgware, Middlesex. Her father retained meticulous accounts and paperwork, leaving Pat with a detailed record of receipts and other household paperwork from the 1930s.

'My father paid £835 for 9, Brook Avenue, Edgware, Middlesex, in 1938. He put down £200 in cash as a deposit and used a mortgage with the then Abbey Road Building Society.'

The monthly repayments were £4 each month for the three-bedroom semi with front and back gardens.

My grandparents thought my father was taking on too much. They said that if anything went wrong in the house, it would have to be paid out of his own pocket. But this did not deter him.

The layout of such a new house would be familiar to anyone who has lived or is still living in a thirties semi in a city suburb. These houses varied from estate to estate, with different styles, i.e. Jacobean-, Georgian- or Tudor-style homes.

Nineteen-thirties house front doors usually had three panels at the bottom and a large glass window at the top, with brass knockers and house numbers on the front. The front door opens to a hallway, from which there are stairs to the upper floor, two doors into the living rooms and at the end of the hall, a door into a kitchen. Upstairs consists of a landing, two bedrooms, plus a smaller box bedroom and a bathroom sited above the kitchen. There is also a sizeable loft above the upper floor.

Room sizes varied; some 1930s houses had chalet-type roofs, meaning smaller loft areas. Some windows – which were single-glazed in those days – were attractive rounded bays, some square and others had no bay at all, though bay windows tended to be a big feature of 1930s homes – in a way, a mark of home ownership.

Houses tended to be smaller in the less affluent new estates but they were all to a similar general pattern, inside and out.

Inside the hallway, the owners would usually place a hat stand and a small table for letters or other post. New linoleum (also known as 'lino') flooring in the house gave the impression of tiling – but without the cost.

Kitchens painted in cream or duck-egg blue were fashionable to complement the large ceramic sink and new gas cooker. Interior doors were often also painted in the same colours to match the kitchen.

Living rooms had chintz curtains, with throws over the 1930s three-piece suite. Oak and mahogany tables were fashionable too, though the cheaper plywood tended to be more common.

One of the biggest complaints about these family suburban semis came from those living in the estates with smaller houses. The semis had a shared side entrance with the house next door. Gardens were quite small too on this type of estate, so in later post-war years, with car ownership growing, many families opted to build a garage in the back-garden area.

Inside the 1938 house, Pat Cryer remembers floors covered with lino: 'The hall was dark brown linoleum in a marble pattern, my mother would polish it until it shone.'

The other floor coverings were also dark brown apart from the front bedroom, which was pale green, brighter than the other rooms. Pat still has her father's estimate for the cost of new lino: £12 17 shillings for all floor coverings, apart from the front room.

The bathroom and lavatory floors in their house were

black and white lino tiles, with matching black and white ceramic wall tiles – a very typical 1930s bathroom.

'My mother Florence used to call the lino "oil cloth". This was a heavy-duty cloth to create a wipe-over surface, which would have been the norm in Victorian terraces where she grew up. Oil cloth and lino were very similar,' says Pat.

Coal was essentially the only form of heating in these new houses. Gas fires were lit very rarely. A boiler in the kitchen heated all the water, making the kitchen very cosy. The boiler was fed on coke.

Insurance for the contents of the Brook Avenue semi from the Prudential Assurance Company for a 'hearth and home' policy totalled £1,500 in July 1938.

Transport, of course, played a crucial role in the development of the new housing estates and suburbs, with their rows of semis. Many new houses were built alongside the arterial roads that led into and out of the large cities – ribbon development – but while car ownership in the thirties was very low by today's standards (just over three million private cars and motorcycles on the roads in 1938), the development of the new suburbs owed much to easy access to public transport, the trolley buses, trams and coaches now travelling on the roads. The advantage of the house in Brook Avenue was that it was a seven-minute walk from Edgware tube station – which had already benefited from the extension of the underground Northern Line to Edgware in 1924.

As for the onset of war for families like Pat's, who had only recently started paying off their mortgage commitment, all mortgage repayments were briefly suspended in 1939 for those families where men were joining the armed forces. After war was officially declared, a Government Hardship Committee offered help for people who couldn't afford to pay their rents or mortgages and this, along with building societies opting to suspend capital payments (so that mortgagees paid interest only for a period of time), or to lengthen mortgage terms for those either on active service or whose livelihood or income was affected by the war, helped most of the new home-buyers to avoid losing their properties.

The rise in employment and wage levels during the war, with many women, of all ages, working long shifts in the factories to support the war effort, meant that thousands of mortgages were, in fact, paid off early – and repossession levels were very low.

The ribbon development of new houses around the main roads outside the cities was a key planning issue. The Metropolitan Green Belt was first proposed by the Greater London Regional Planning Committee in 1935 in order to curb urban sprawl and keep some land permanently open. Yet it was not until 1947 that local authorities all over the country were permitted to include green-belt proposals in all their development plans.

6

WORKING LIFE

By the late 1930s, while living standards were improving for those with work in the South and Midlands, the long-term effect of the leaner years of the 1920s and the early 1930s continued to keep unemployment levels high.

Certainly, new jobs in the North were emerging. One good example is a former cotton mill in Blackburn, the Garden Street Mill. This became a gas-mask assembly plant in 1937, with a capacity to manufacture half a million gas masks a week.

That same year, a new Royal Ordnance Factory making fuses for munitions opened nearby and another Blackburn company, Mullard's in Little Harwood, became a mainstay of local employment for both sexes when the company started developing a plant making electronic components on a brand-new industrial estate. Initially, the plant manufactured radio valves, but by the end of 1938, further expansion brought large-scale production of electronic components, especially for military systems.

War changed Britain's job market. Unemployment in the UK was over 10 per cent in 1939, but by 1941, with so many men enlisted in the armed forces or working in reserved occupations, there was an official shortage of two million workers.

Millions of pairs of hands were urgently needed for paid jobs in the armaments and munitions factories across the country. Some of these factories had to be built from scratch, in semi-secret locations, many others were set up in requisitioned buildings: everyone in them worked round the clock, producing everything the country needed to support the war effort. Tanks, planes, guns, bullets, bombs, parachutes, uniforms . . . these factory workers became crucial in helping to build up the country's defences.

Given the choice of going into the armed forces, the Land Army or opting for factory work late in 1941 (when conscription for women was finally introduced), a new breed of young, unmarried, working-class women – many still in their teens, some who had never had jobs before – began working in the factories.

The shifts would be long and the routine often relentless, yet their weekly pay packet was a big improvement on what they had previously earned if they had already been working in service or at a shop counter.

Shopkeepers in the 1930s sought to reduce labour costs

by recruiting large numbers of young people on low wages. By 1931, two in five shop assistants were under twenty-one. By the mid-1930s, 10 per cent of the country's young wage-earners were working as shop assistants. School-leavers could also find work in low-paid jobs, for instance as errand boys or as live-out domestic workers.

Domestic work 'in service' in big houses and on country estates had been on the decline since the First World War. By 1931, only 5 per cent of households in England and Wales could boast resident domestic help, and attempts to encourage younger women into service in the 1920s (with organised homecraft courses) fell flat. There were still upper- and middle-class households willing to keep one or two low-paid, live-out servants as part of their household running costs, but by then, most younger women preferred the option of shop or factory work, even if the pay was low, rather than living in the somewhat restrictive situation of being a live-in servant with all its attendant rules.

Jobs for women in the 'new' industries – for instance, the production lines in the big factories producing the new mass-manufactured consumer goods like toys, clothing and domestic appliances – also had a positive impact on the labour market for young people, as did new legislation. The Factories Acts of 1937 and 1938 limited juvenile hours of work to nine hours a day, and a total of forty-four hours a week.

Essentially, it was the retail and service industries that provided much of the employment for young people.

As cities and big towns expanded alongside increasing transport options in the later part of the 1930s, so too did the numbers of shops and department stores, all needing unskilled workers to serve the ever-growing numbers of shoppers. The department stores, more upmarket emporiums, tended to offer higher wages than the smaller shops.

High-street retail names familiar in Britain even today, like Marks & Spencer, Sainsbury's, John Lewis, Selfridges, Boots and the Co-op, had been in existence before 1930. Like the manufacturing industries, they too underwent a great deal of expansion in the decade before the Second World War. Additionally, the 1930s housing boom, as outlined in the previous chapter, provided a big boost in employment levels, doubling the numbers of unskilled working men needed as labourers and providing greater job opportunities for skilled specialists like glaziers, electricians, plasterers, tilers, plumbers and carpenters.

Overall, the impact of all this gives a quite different picture of a country that had previously languished in the throes of the Depression era. It was the beginning – albeit in a class-divided nation that was still a very unequal society – of the consumer world of the present day.

As the writer J. B. Priestley (1894–1984) observed as he travelled around England in the late 1930s:

This is the England of arterial and bypass roads and factories that look like exhibition buildings, of giant cinemas and dance halls and cafés, bungalows with tiny garages, cocktail bars, Woolworths, motor coaches, wireless, hiking, factory girls like actresses, greyhound racing and dirt tracks, swimming pools and everything given away for cigarette coupons ...

This more affluent, consumer-led society with its attendant glamour is also reflected in the day-to-day working environment of fifteen-year-old Bert Hollick. Bert's first job in 1935, working on the railway network on the lowest rung of the pecking order, was at a time when a twelve- to fourteen-hour working day was still commonplace. His starting wage was just £2 a week, providing a luxury service to travellers on the Pullman car *Brighton Belle*, the famous London-to-Brighton rail service (UK Pullman trains were mainline luxury railway services operating with first-class coaches and a steward service on board).

Bert's description of life as a Pullman attendant from his first day onwards provides a fascinating insight: 'I was employed by the Pullman Company and during my four years on the railway as an attendant, I travelled thousands of miles on the various routes run by the then Southern Railway.'

On his first day, Bert reported to the company's office at Brighton station and was issued with a pass allowing him to travel anywhere on the Southern Region. He then had to report to the Pullman head office at Victoria station, where he was measured for his uniform, a dark blue jacket with gold braiding around the lapels and cuffs, and gold buttons. The trousers were dark blue with a blue stripe down each outer leg, plus a similar-coloured peaked cap with gold braid on the peak and a band with PULLMAN CAR CO. around it. He was provided with a new uniform every year; the peaked cap was always worn inside or outside the car. 'My salary was £2 a week plus tips, on average 3d or 6d a time. All the tips were pooled and the attendant in charge would share them out.'

After a week's training, Bert was detailed to his first Pullman car, named *Bertha*: 'On the Southern, all trains were electrified. Apart from the all-Pullman *Brighton Belle*, there were twenty electric Pullmans, numbering 1–20, all possessing female Christian names. Each Pullman unit would be in the middle of a six-coach corridor train.'

Serving packed trainloads of day-trippers or theatregoers with food and drink on the Pullman as it went up and down to the coast was usually a hard slog.

The Brighton to Victoria shift meant 4.25pm up to London, 6pm down to Brighton, 7.25pm up, 9pm down, 10.25pm up, midnight down, arriving in Brighton around 1am. Then you'd be up to the siding to clear up, check stock, finally getting home to sleep at 2.30am. After the 9pm down, one would feel worn out, but you still had two very busy trips ahead. The midnight train from Victoria was the busiest of all the trips, full of theatregoers all wanting drinks after a night out.

There were no overtime payments. Quite often, a planned free evening would vanish if there was a breakdown elsewhere and Bert's shift would be suddenly extended. Working in the Pullman car on the *Brighton Belle*, Bert was one of a crew of four:

The chef, who always had to have whites on, along with a chef's hat, an attendant in charge, an assistant serving in the car, and an attendant just serving refreshments on the other plain coaches up the corridor. On a busy train the attendant had to carry three trays, two on the right hand and arm, one in the left hand. Very seldom any breakages, even at a train speed of 75mph.

On arrival at London, a Pullman motor van would unload stores, ordered the previous day, to the unit concerned. No frozen foods then, all fresh vegetables, meat, etc., all from the main depot at Battersea. Clean linen delivered every day, table cloths, napkins and hand towels. Soiled linen was returned to the Battersea depot and laundered.

On the early turns, we'd serve breakfasts, porridge, fruit juice, kippers, bacon and eggs – poached, scrambled or boiled – toast and marmalade, tea or coffee.

The busiest lunch turn was the 1pm Victoria to Brighton, arriving at 1.58pm. Food was prepared by the chef during earlier trips. Menu would start with hors d'oeuvres or soup (served from a tureen) – no easy task on a train travelling at 75mph. Then there could be fish (halibut or Dover sole), roast chicken, chops, cutlets or mixed grill, all with three vegetables. Sweets were Charlotte Russe [a classic Edwardian dessert, a type of trifle consisting of sponge fingers, fruit and custard], fruit salad or apple tart with cream, steamed apple pudding with sauces, baked jam roll with sauce. Then cheese and biscuits and coffee.

While the price of breakfast was 2 shillings and 6 pence, this four-course lunch was priced at 3 shillings and 6 pence. Drinks cost 6 pence for a nip of whisky or gin, while brandy was 1 shilling and 6 pence per nip. Cigars were either 1 shilling and 6 pence or 2 shillings.

'We had fifty-eight minutes to serve drinks and a four-course lunch with silver service and coffee and then to collect the cash from about forty passengers. A good system was vital. Unless you worked to a system, it could be chaotic.'

On extra-busy shifts, it did turn chaotic:

The chef would sometimes get into a flap, burning the soup, dropping a dish of vegetables and so on. He had a lot of work on, what with the service taking place in the car and the corridor attendant shouting orders to him. In summer, the galley became a sweat box. Against company rules the vestibule doors would be clipped back, letting in a rush of air from the speed of the train. Noisy, but very cooling for the chef! ['Vestibule' is the term used for the area at each end of a railway carriage, where the external doors are.]

In the Pullman car, serving coffee could be a nightmare:

> With a silver jug of coffee in one hand and a similar jug
> of hot milk in the other, one would start to pour and mix
> the milk and coffee when the train would lurch over a
> slight curve of track and instead of finding the coffee cup,
> known as a demitasse, one would find the passenger's lap.
> After travelling the tracks for many months, the average
> attendant knew just where any curves, bends and sharp
> points occurred.

Staff were not allowed to consume the food stocks aboard, except cups of tea: 'The usual procedure was to dash out on arriving at the destination, purchase chops, vegetables, etc., and the chef would then prepare us a meal, either for consumption in the sidings or en route. Staff were not allowed to drink on duty, but it still went on – a drink could be obtained any time of the day once the train was on the move.'

The Pullman car consisted of a kitchen, including electric stove, grill and oven, store cupboards, a hot-water urn, a sink and crockery. Alongside was the ice safe or box (refrigerators were available for sale in the late 1930s, price around £22, but the ice safe, where big blocks of ice were kept in an insulated box with hollow walls, was in fairly common use in pre-war catering). Next to the kitchen there was a pantry with crockery, silver, glasses, wines, spirits, beers and expensive cigars. Kitchen waste was emptied from bins aboard into incinerators at depots. No ashtrays were to be emptied out of windows – a lit cigarette end could blow back into an empty compartment and start a fire.

Seating on a first-class Pullman car was twelve comfortable armchair seats with antimacassars (a decorative cloth placed on the back of the seats to protect them from dirt or grease – most typically from hair oil [Macassar oil] commonly used by men at the time), glass-topped tables with brass lamps and ashtrays. There was also a separate private cubicle with seating for VIPs. If a passenger required anything, he or she would press a bell push by the seat and the number of the seat light up red.

Accommodation in third-class Pullman carriages (effectively, second-class travel or standard as we know it today, but for confusing reasons third-class rail travel was only officially rebadged as second class by the then British Railways in 1956) consisted of sixteen seats, four at a table, again with a glass top, ashtray and table lamp, but this was ordinary, less luxurious seating.

Various light refreshments could also be delivered on trays by Pullman staff to passengers in compartments, served on tables fitted into the compartment. There were supplementary charges for this service, between 2 shillings (in first class) and 1 shilling and 6 pence (in third class). A pot of tea and toast or biscuits cost 9d; coffee and biscuits 10d.

In his four years with Pullman, Bert found himself

serving many wealthy or well-known people, including royalty travelling on the Pullman train to a function or to the races.

Red carpeting was laid along the platform, right up to the entrance to the Pullman car. I saw Her Majesty Queen Elizabeth [as she was then, subsequently HM the Queen Mother, who died in 2002, aged one hundred and one].

I saw her at a very close distance and was surprised to see how much her features were made up cosmetically. Only the conductor would be allowed to make any contact with the royal party.

Other well-known passengers Bert served included stage and screen celebrities like the singer and actress Gracie Fields, the Crazy Gang (a very popular group of six comedians, including Bud Flanagan and Chesney Allen, whose popularity extended beyond the Second World War into the late 1950s), Tommy Farr (one of the UK's most celebrated heavyweight boxers) and the comedian Max Miller (known as 'the Cheeky Chappie' for his somewhat risqué repertoire).

'Many stage stars and wealthy people would come on, leaving the porter to load their luggage into the vestibule of the Pullman car, perhaps eight or ten pieces of luggage piled on top of each other.'

The Crazy Gang were regulars, arriving direct from performances at the London Palladium: 'They'd get on at

11.30pm, occupy a private enclosure, hand over steaks or whatever to the chef, tip him and by the time the train was due out, they'd have had their meal and then the table would be cleared and they'd settle down to play cards.'

Serving royalty and celebrities was one thing, but other journeys were not without incident. Sometimes drunken fights would break out in the corridors or compartments, with windows and lights broken. At those times, the train would stop at the next signal box, the information would be passed on and at the next station, police would board the train.

The Company had a lot of trouble with race gangs. Race specials were part of Pullman service, sometimes not very profitable and after the racing, many racegoers were drunk on getting aboard. This was the era of the razor gangs [razor-wielding young men usually involved in racketeering at racecourses in the 1930s and 1940s].

One drunken racegoer, big and rough, demanded a seat in the Pullman. Staff tried to ease him into the corridor but he pushed his way into the car, picking up teapots and smashing tabletops.

All hell was let loose, an attendant pulled the communication cord and the train halted.

The driver and guard came along the track, phoned police from a box and on arriving at Haywards Heath station, police came aboard and took him off the train.

During the rumpus, not one racegoer or bookie had raised a hand to control this person.

Part of Bert's job involved canvassing compartments in order to sell refreshments. This too had its hazards.

Very often an attendant, including myself, would open a compartment door with all the blinds pulled down and surprise a loving couple, well into the throes of lovemaking.

I canvassed Max Miller in a first-class compartment and embarrassed him at the same time by finding him in a compromising position with his secretary – she travelled with him quite a lot.

On one occasion, on a Friday night on the 5.25pm Victoria to Brighton run, Bert canvassed a first-class compartment to find a businessman, truly the worse for drink, with a gorgeous female.

Sitting next to the man she had both breasts outside her dress and he was fondling her. Strange as it may seem, there were other businessmen in the same compartment but the female didn't seem too bothered. Another of those dirty weekends in Brighton, which were the talk of the day.

Long hours aside, however, Bert enjoyed his time on the Pullman car. In 1939, along with many others in the crew he worked with, he was called up.

Alas, some crew members were to lose their lives in the war. Time moved on and after the war, The Pullman Car Co. came to an end. Some of the cars were scrapped, others sold as caravans, small cafés, summer houses and various other modes of use.

Gone is the glory of first-class service, of comfort and good food – never to be seen again on the Southern region of the railways.

A DESK JOB

A clerical job offered twenty-two-year-old Londoner Eric Phillips a somewhat less energetic role for £2 and 10 shillings a week. He had spotted an advertisement for the job in a newspaper, the *News Chronicle*, in 1937. His membership of the London Trades Council (an early labour organisation campaigning to improve working conditions) proved helpful in getting the job (from 1935–9, trade union membership had risen 39 per cent to 6.2 million, one million of whom were female).

The ad was for an estate clerk in the London County Council's Valuation, Estates and Housing Department. It said: 'A knowledge of building methods would be an advantage.' I applied and I remember it had about four blank pages for you to write about your experience in building. As I didn't have very much at all, I just put the word 'slight' on the first page and on the subsequent pages, I said, 'See page one'.

Of course I got the inevitable answer: 'Thank you for your application but at the moment, etc.' But twenty-four hours later, it was followed by another letter which said, would I please arrange to come for an interview.

He was interviewed by the sub-committee of the Housing Committee. 'They were rather helpful as I was a delegate to the London Trades Council and had got the secretary to stand as a referee. The other referee was my trade union organiser and as it was a Labour-run council, it went down fairly well.'

Eric got the job, estate clerk on the Becontree Estate, in Dagenham, Essex – a very large council-run cottage housing estate, completed in 1935 with 26,000 homes housing over 100,000 people. The estate was one of thirteen new cottage estates built by the London County Council between 1919 and 1939.

That first Monday, I got there early at the Estate Office at 100 Ford Road. I was met by the superintendent of the section, who was a lovely gentleman – he made me most welcome. The office opened at half past nine. There was another clerk there and the superintendent showed me what I had to do.

He said: 'There's the rent book and there's the squares with the dates against them. You put down the amount and you enter it on a sheet of paper, which is headed with the name of the road. You put the number of the house and the amount you've taken. There's £5 worth of change over there, sort it out in the till here.'

'Then he said, 'Oh, I've got to open the office now.' And that was the extent of my training.

Becontree was divided up into twenty-one sections with an estate office in each one of them. The rent offices were graded from 1 to 4, with 4 being the smallest. Eric worked in a Grade 1 office, which consisted of a Grade 1 clerk, two estate clerks and a superintendent living in a cottage adjacent to the office.

We would take 800 rents every week. At the end of the week, we then did a balancing trick with the figures, put it down on a sheet of paper and sent it up to the central office at 882 Green Lane, Dagenham.

There was an iron grille between me and the customers and they would push their rent book and the cash underneath the grille. The grille was there so if anyone got irate about something, they couldn't jump at you over the counter. If there wasn't much of a queue, one or two people would have a chat with me. A very few were abusive but otherwise people were reasonable and I think we were too.

Afternoons were for new lettings:

That was when someone came along to view a cottage. Most of the people took what was offered to them. You issued them with a rent book and there was a 5-shilling key deposit, which was refundable if they moved out, providing 5 shillings' worth of damage – for instance, broken windows – had not taken place.

Another part of the job was serving Notice to Quit:

If people were a week in arrears with their rent, we would send a 'First Arrears Letter', which would be a gentle reminder. If it continued for another two or three weeks, you would send a second letter of rather sterner stuff: 'Look here, you've got to pull yourself together and get paid up or else!'

If there was no effort being made, you would serve a Notice to Quit. This was merely a safeguard in case it went on and on. If the rent didn't get paid, they would end up in court.

As I recall, there were very few evictions during my couple of years before the war. Usually the family would skedaddle, leave without giving their notice. Possibly there'd been a family dispute or he or she fancied the bottle too much or had got into debt on the horses, having used the rent to back the next winner that lost!

Behind Eric's office was a yard which housed a carpenter, plumber, handyman and a few decorators.

People would come in, reporting repairs to us and after we had balanced up in the afternoon, we would issue chits [a short note recording work to be done or a sum of money] for the workmen. Usually there was quite a lapse between asking for a job to be done and it being executed because demand exceeded the human resources to meet it. Another job we had was to show people the wallpaper book, which had about half a dozen patterns in it. If a house was due for decoration [every five years the council would decorate a house from top to bottom], they could choose which wallpaper they wanted. The Grade 1 clerk was then responsible for issuing instructions to the decorators and he would make out a schedule.

Eric was on probation for the first year in the job: 'After that, it was the beginning of my forty-odd years with the London County Council and the Greater London Council.'

RENTING ON THE BECONTREE ESTATE

In 1933, the weekly rents, including water charges and rates, on the Becontree Estate were listed as follows:

Two Room Flat: 9/6d a week
Three Room Flat: 11/6d a week
Three Room Cottage: 12/6d a week
Four Room Cottage: 14 shillings–15/6d a week
Five Room Cottage: 17/6d a week
Six Room Cottage: 22/6d a week

Each cottage or flat had a garden, front and back, with gas installed. In addition, electricity for lighting was installed in many of the homes.

In areas where jobs were still extremely hard to come by, it was frequently a parent or sibling who would endeavour to shoehorn a school-leaver into work.

Betty Nettle's story is typical. Born in 1925, she grew up in a coal-mining area near Stormy Down, Bridgend, South Wales. The youngest of six children, her father worked on the local railway as a ganger – a foreman of a group of labourers.

> Work round where I lived was very scarce before the war. My older sisters went into service up in London, the only work option for girls then. Families were big too, so if a family in our area had a shop, then their children or young relatives worked in it.
>
> Work was all about who you knew, not what you knew.

Betty left school aged fourteen in July 1939: 'My mother said to me, "There's a job going at Kenfig Hill [a nearby village], minding a little one-year-old baby, start Monday."'

So, Betty finished school on the Friday and started work the following Monday. Her mother had arranged everything, as she knew the family for whom Betty would be working.

The pay was half a crown (2 shillings and 6 pence) a

week, starting at around 7am and finishing around 6pm, with a half-day on Saturday and Sunday mornings free. 'The family had a drapers' shop – in the front room of their house – but they sold all sorts of things.'

Betty liked the baby, 'a real little doll'. She would get him up in the morning, wash him, dress him, feed him and take him out for a walk in a big boat pram.

The day war broke out in September 1939 was certainly a most unhappy memory.

My mother was crying, she'd lost a brother in the First War. There was an aerodrome a few miles away and we knew they were constructing a brand-new arsenal [a Royal Ordnance munitions factory] at Bridgend because my brother Jack was already working there, helping to build it. He'd worked in quarries but once word got round that the arsenal paid better money than the quarries, off he went to work there.

The new Bridgend munitions site had been chosen because it was remote from other areas vulnerable to enemy bombing, yet reasonably close to three major ports and had a plentiful supply of unemployed labour.

Betty continued to look after the baby for the next eighteen months. Then she switched to another child-minding job, this time looking after two children in the next village, a live-in job with a farming family – until the workload got too much.

I just left, went home and stayed there. Then one day, my sister Mary said: "They're taking on youngsters at the arsenal" and my ears pricked up. Mary was already working there and she had money to spend – which I didn't.

The money was good – £2 a week, a lot more than I'd been getting. I had so little from the childminding, I'd walk home from the first job to save thruppence [3d] to put towards things I'd save up for, like clothes.

At first, Betty worked in the textiles section of the huge arsenal, the largest single-site munitions factory in the UK, employing 40,000 people. Initially, she worked on a sewing machine, making workers' uniforms, turbans, waistcoats and trousers.

At the age of eighteen, she was transferred to the filling section. Here, the work was dangerous: making pellets for propellant, using different types of powdered explosive. Moving to pellets, however, meant shift work and a fatter wage packet. Later on, she would help assemble rockets, fitting the nose cones onto the projectiles.

In an area like Bridgend, which had known serious hardship through the 1920s and 1930s, wartime was as tough as it was elsewhere, yet for younger women like Betty it brought a regular wage packet they could never have earned in peacetime.

'I don't care what anyone says, the main reason Bridgend was so popular with everyone working there was the money. A few of the girls at the arsenal were bringing home more money than their fathers – though they didn't dare tell them.'

Like Betty Nettle, Joyce Storey left school, at Kingswood, near Bristol, at the age of fourteen. She too found herself being shoehorned into her first job in 1931 via a friend of her mother's called Lottie, who ran a local drapery store. Lottie had some relatives, a family running a modest shop, who needed live-in help.

Lottie made much of the job, glossing it over so that it sounded the chance of a lifetime. I was to receive five shillings a week – she mentioned the five bob first. She was quite right – I had never had five bob in the whole of my life. My duties would be simple, she said, merely helping in the house, with a bit of cooking and light cleaning. There was a little girl to be fetched from school, but I would be very happy there; she just knew that I would get on with her brother Harold and his wife, and of course I would get good food, the best.

My mother made me a blue velvet holdall with brown bone handles. She also made me a flannelette nightie and a skirt with two warm blouses. I started my duties the following Monday.

Harold was tall and freckly and he had a boyish face. He respected his customers and wanted only to do the best by them, so he had a friendly and pleasing manner. His wife was different: she also was tall and slim but with a haughty attitude. She looked down on me now, and although her smile was as bright as a 60-watt lamp, I could tell she was asking herself if this tiny slip of a girl could get through a rota of duties she had in mind for her. She quickly made a decision and spoke to me.

'I shall require you to help with the preparation of the meals, the washing-up and clearing away. There will, of course, be a certain amount of cleaning to be done and I shall allocate your various duties daily. I have a daughter who needs to be fetched from school and you will be required to play with her until bedtime. There will be a small amount of mending and sewing to be done, but shall we give it a trial, say, for a month? See how we get on?'

She then showed me a little box room that contained a bed and a small bedside cabinet, but outside on the landing was a cupboard which she said I could use to hang my things and a shelf above was also at my disposal. The cupboard had a musty smell.

I found nothing difficult in the work I had to do in the days that followed. I loved the little girl and read to her and played with her for hours. Only one thing worried me: I came down one morning to find that Mrs Collins had put a duckboard [a slatted wooden board, placed to form a path over muddy ground] to stand on to start the washing. The big tub stood on a long bench. Even with the duckboard, I could hardly see over the top and the heat and steam made me feel hot and faint. At home, I might have helped turn the mangle [a mechanical laundry aid consisting of two rollers to wring out water from clothes] or held the sheets and helped my mother hang things on the line, but I had never actually had to do all the washing by myself. All done by hand, of course: shirts, overalls, tablecloths, towels, sheets, the lot. That night I fell into bed sick with exhaustion.

Joyce had a half-day off every Thursday afternoon: 'One day I took a walk down Castle Street and then I saw it: a coat with a great fur collar that would make me look like a film star. The more I looked at it, the more convinced I became that I must have it.'

The coat was priced at £2 and 10 shillings. Joyce arranged to pay for it in instalments of 5 shillings a time and once the last instalment was paid, she could collect the coat.

Every Thursday after that, I went to the shop and paid my 5 shillings off. One more payment only now remained and this Thursday, I would be collecting it. I skipped through the bedrooms. I sang as I flipped the duster lightly over the ornaments. The vegetables were ready and standing in salted water and the meat was in the roasting tin surrounded by the potatoes that were to be baked for supper. Lunch was cold meat and salad, which I intended to miss because of wanting to be out on the dot.

At exactly ten minutes to two, Joyce presented herself for her wages.

Mrs Collins hesitated, then looked at her watch. She glanced up at the big clock on the wall.

'Ah now,' she said and my heart sank, 'there is a small job I would like you to do before you go. Then I will have your money ready for you and you can be away. I would like the coal cellar to be washed over. Put the house flannel on the end of the broom, but give it a good sweeping first.'

'It never occurred to me to refuse her. I just stood there in abject misery, knowing it would mean having to take off all my decent clothes and then afterwards wash before I could go out. It would be three o'clock before I would be out of the house on my precious half-day.'

Joyce suddenly became very angry:

I would wash her bloody floor like it had never been washed before. I cannot remember getting the pail or the water but I began to scrub each patch slowly and methodically. I didn't feel the stone floor tear and ladder the only pair of black silk stockings I possessed. My face was smudged with coal dust and tears; my black dress, where the water had dripped down the front, was stained and filthy. It was only when I came to the final patch that I looked up and swore a terrible oath: 'This is the last time in my entire bloody life I will ever be on my knees with my nose to the ground, for I belong up there with my eyes to the light, and walking upright and tall.'

Joyce completed her task and walked upstairs.

> Mrs Collins opened her mouth to say something when she saw the state I was in, but took a step backward when she saw the wild glint in my eyes that held the clear message that our paths would never meet again. She held out my five shillings and I passed her without a word. I had worked blindly and solidly for this woman for ten weeks, for a coat I was now going to collect, come hell or high water.
>
> I must have looked a sight with my coal-black face, my stockings all torn and my hair dishevelled and with that dreadful determined look on my face. Even the shop assistant ran to collect the package when I demanded to have it now and not a moment later.

Joyce returned home to Kingswood:

> When I opened the door of our sitting room, my mother as usual was on the sewing machine. She watched me fling myself into an armchair and sob, hard sobs that tore at my insides and made it difficult to breathe. She waited until I had quietened down, then with a long sigh she said, 'I'll go and make us a nice cup of tea, girl.'

By the mid-1930s, in densely populated urban areas where there were plenty of shops of all kinds, young women found they could easily secure work behind a shop counter – and sometimes move around from job to job.

WORKING LIFE

Marjorie Gardiner was fifteen when she decided to work in millinery, encouraged by her sister-in-law, who had worked in that trade (the wearing of hats by both sexes was at its peak in the 1920s and 1930s, but started to decline in the post-war years).

Marjorie's first job was in a very small, exclusive shop in the Seven Dials area of Brighton:

I suppose in those days I was very fashion-conscious. The shop window had silk drapes and was dressed with one gown, one hat and a vase of real flowers, beautifully arranged. All was changed every few days and everything had to be of the very best.

There was only Madam and myself as the apprentice. Madam was a lovely lady, very kind and quite young, perhaps in her late twenties. The wage was 2 shillings and 6 pence a week for the first year and 3 shillings and 6 pence thereafter.

Marjorie remained in the job for three years until her employer married a tea planter and went to live abroad. The shop was sold.

I then applied for a post of junior sales assistant in a very high-class millinery establishment. I was chosen out of a number of applicants – Madam had given me an excellent reference – and my new Madam was big and blonde, somewhat in the style of Mae West. I had heard she was a tyrant but it was not easy to get a job and I was thankful for the offer.

This was a different world from Marjorie's previous job, rigid rules and discipline replacing the relaxed atmosphere she'd known. However, the other girls were friendly, which made a difference.

The shop had two very big showrooms, one downstairs and one upstairs. Above the latter was the workroom, where the head milliner and four girls were kept busy all day, making hats and working on alterations and trimmings. The workroom consisted of the head milliner, two under-milliners and an apprentice whose job it was to run errands, get ribbons and other materials needed for hats being made for customers; she went out in all weathers.

Hats were made in those days from wire shapes or on a varnished wooden block covered by buckram, a kind of net stiffened and dried to the needed shape. Customers who had hats made came in for a fitting before they were completed, as they had to be just what the customer ordered. And the milliners also had to account for their time on the work. Although some hats were made to order or altered by these shop milliners, most hats came from the wholesalers.

The showroom consisted of four or five long counters with hat stands which had to be dressed out each day, with toning coloured hats chosen by the senior assistants, helped by the juniors, who fetched and brushed the ones needed. The apprentices had to bring artificial flowers and feathers for decorating the hats, making them look individual.

The shop opened at 9am, but at 8.30am, a stream of smart young ladies, all dressed in black, filed through the back entrance of the shop and went up the stairs to a shabby cloakroom. Here, we would put a last touch to our hair and faces, took off our outdoor shoes and replaced them with black, high-heeled satin ones. By nine o'clock, the door was open and even in winter remained open through the day, no matter how bitter the weather. The hours were long, 9am to 7pm Monday, Tuesday Wednesday, on Friday night we were supposed to leave at 8pm and on Saturday, 9pm but we were not free even then if there were still customers around.

In those days shop assistants always wore black dresses, mostly black satin in summer and velvet in winter:

A little while later, we were allowed a touch of white, such as a little collar or a frilly front, known as a jabot. No jewellery was permitted, apart from a wristwatch and an engagement ring, if appropriate.

When we were busy, we had to serve two or three customers at a time but however busy we were, as soon as someone came through the doorway, we had to greet her and find her a chair to sit on while she was waiting, apologising for the delay and assuring her she would be attended to as soon as possible. In those days, 'the customer is always right' meant precisely that and we were never allowed to forget it.

Millinery for women in mourning made up a big part of the shop's business, as Marjorie recalled:

Widows' weeds, a black hat draped with black veiling, were almost compulsory when I first went into the business. Widows wore them to their husband's funeral with the veil over their faces and continued to wear them for several months afterwards. 'Weeds' then went out of fashion but we continued to do a tremendous trade in black hats as everyone who went into mourning wore black, from head to toe. It was only when clothes rationing started in the Second World War that this custom started to die out.

When King George V died in 1936, buyers from everywhere were dashing to buy up every available black hat from the manufacturers as nearly everyone, it seemed, wanted a black hat for his funeral and windows everywhere were draped in black.

When war broke out, Marjorie went to work in another milliner's. 'I was now married and continued in my job until the end of the war. Life was now getting easier for shop girls. The hours were not so long and the pay was increasing a little, but it was never very good. Even when I was manageress of a shop my wages, until the day I left, were only £3 a week and commission.'

WORKING LIFE

Maisie Jagger was born in 1922 in Woolwich, South-East London, and grew up in Essex, where her father had bought a house on a new estate.

I was one of five, two boys and three girls. We were a very close-knit family, that's for sure.

At the top end of our road there were quite a few shops. I left school at fourteen and went straight into shop work. I was never once out of work. I think I worked in every shop near us: a grocer's shop first, then a shop called Perk Stores, then a shop called Gunners – they had biscuits in tins all along the front of the shop.

I worked on the counter of a fish-and-chip shop and I also worked in a place called Maypole. I can remember the cheese they sold, covered with something like a sack, a type of webbing all around it.

I was quite a friendly girl. You had to get on with everyone in the shop, didn't you? But I'd also change jobs quickly for a penny or tuppence more a week. By the time war broke out, I was working as a machinist, making haversacks and binocular cases in a big factory.

Whatever I earned went straight to Mum on a Thursday – when I knew she wouldn't have any money left until Dad got paid on Friday night. In return, I'd get 6 pence a week as pocket money.

Alice Reynolds started her working life at the age of fourteen as a shop assistant in a department store in Hove,

East Sussex. Her pay was 25 shillings a week plus a sales commission of 3 pence in the £1.

In 1936, she was increasingly bored at work:

> I decided to do something about it. I went to the local labour exchange to see if there was another job I could do that would be more fulfilling.
>
> The counter clerk said: 'Have you thought of becoming a nurse?'
>
> 'No.'
>
> 'Take this form and go and see the matron of Southlands Hospital at Shoreham. She'll be very pleased to see you – she is very short of nurses.'

At Southlands, Alice went to meet the matron.

'"Good morning," she said. "Sit down, Nurse."

'Now whether she automatically called everyone "Nurse" or whether it was a ploy to help the applicant make up her mind, I didn't know. But it certainly made up mine!'

The job involved three years' training: 'I like the Irish girls best because they can't run home,' said the Matron. (Later, Alice discovered that it took the Irish girls all year to save the £5 required for their fare home.)

The work meant living in at the nurses' home:

> From being a nobody, I was now a somebody. I had my own room; hot baths whenever I needed or felt inclined; a blue and white uniform, starched caps and aprons and very good

food served in the dining room. Maids brought round dishes of vegetables and there were glasses and jugs of water. It was all very different from home – maids made our beds and cleaned our rooms!

My wages were 25 shillings a month, which also had to cover buying text and exercise books and stockings, but we all managed as everything else was there for us.

My first morning on the wards was strange. Another nurse, Sister Penny, came to my room to help me with my uniform; for a headdress we had a hemstitched bordered cloth, an oblong shape, which, when folded on the long side and pinned onto the hair would be flared out on the head. It was then gathered at the back and pinned with a long safety pin and fanned out into two tails at the back. This made a very fetching headdress! We also wore blue dresses with white aprons, black stockings and black shoes. I felt very smart.

I went on to Men's Medical Ward, A2, not knowing what to expect. I was hailed from a bed and approached the patient's side.

'Can I have a bottle?'

I turned to another patient, who was up and about. 'What does he want the bottle for?' I asked innocently.

'Are you new?' the 'up' patient asked. I nodded.

'Come with me,' he said.

Alice was led to the sluice room, where the man showed her a rack of glass male urinals and a pile of nice clean cloths.

'Take a bottle, cover it with a cloth and take it to that patient in bed. When he has used it, cover it again with the cloth and take it back to the sluice, empty it and wash it by holding it over the nozzle in the sink. When you've done that, it gets put back in the rack.'

'That's simple,' I said.

'Yes. But just you wait until you get to bed pans!' and laughing heartily, he sat by his bed and picked up his newspaper.

Alice passed her preliminary exam. Part of the exam included bandaging.

I had the dreaded capeline [a bandage that covers the head or an amputation stump, like a cap]. You joined two ends of the bandages together, by sewing them with the join in the centre of the head; using the two bandages crisscross, you could encapsulate the entire head.

Anyway, after all the hard work and effort put in for the exam, I passed. Another nurse accompanied me – we took the exam together – and afterwards, we had the rest of the day off.

Later in the evening, we got back to Southlands and we were called to the operating theatre. A ten-year-old girl had a burst appendix, which in those days was very serious. As she lay on the operating table, she said to me so plaintively, 'I want my mummy!'

I held her hand and said, 'You'll go to sleep for a little while and when you wake up, you'll see your mummy.'

It was all promises, promises. The little girl didn't wake up. She died and it was left to one of the doctors to break the sad news to her mother.

After this, we nurses had to sterilise all the equipment that had been used in the operation and wash down all the walls; there was no time to stop and think about what had happened. It was just all in the day's work – and we got to bed at 4am that morning.

7

ENTERTAINMENT

DREAM PALACES

WHEN WAR BROKE OUT, NINETEEN MILLION CINEMA TICKETS WERE being sold each week across the UK. Throughout the 1930s, going to the cinema – or 'the flicks' or 'the pictures', as they were known in those days, had increasingly become a hugely popular form of entertainment, especially with younger audiences who could easily afford the cheaper seats at 6 or 7 pence a time.

By 1938, following a wave of new cinema building right across the country, there were nearly 5,000 in the UK. The nation was well and truly hooked on the movies. Nor did war diminish or alter the public's once- or twice-weekly habit of going to the cinema. Along with theatres and other places of entertainment, every cinema in Britain was closed immediately after the declaration of war on

3 September. Yet after just two days, a small cinema in Wales defiantly opened its doors. Within three weeks, cinemas across the country were open again, often playing to packed houses. Theatres also reopened for the duration of the war.

By war's end, despite the bombings, blackouts and innumerable wartime deprivations, around thirty million cinema tickets were being sold each week: wartime proved be a golden era for the cinema. Audiences needed their fix of escapism, fantasy, romance and glamour more than ever when the daily grind of wartime Britain seemed to overshadow their very existence. As one cinema historian described the nation's passion for cinema: 'When their homes were hit, they came back next morning with the bomb dust still in their hair and when the cinema was hit, they climbed over the rubble in the street to ask when it would reopen. They were more sharply affected by the film on the screen than by the conditions that reigned outside.'

Through the war, many British cinemas were destroyed by enemy bombs. By 1945, over 300 of them had been destroyed. Yet because the era before the war had been Hollywood's golden age of film, audiences everywhere benefited.

Many of the new cinemas built in Britain in the late 1920s and early 1930s echoed the style of the newly built lavish picture palaces across America – palatial works of architectural art, buildings with exotic decor, plush seats and soft lighting, constructed to entertain huge audiences in comfort.

In Glasgow, Green's Playhouse, built in 1927, could seat more than 4,300 people. London's Brixton Astoria (now a music venue called the 02 Brixton Academy), built in 1929, could seat 4,750; it was described as 'an acre of seats in a garden of dreams'. The Gaumont State Theatre, in Kilburn, North-West London, which opened in 1937, seated 4,004, split between a massive 1,356-seater balcony and an orchestra level which could seat 2,648.

Until the era of new cinema building, most UK cinemas had been small, outdated affairs, jokingly referred to as 'fleapits'. The newly built cinemas, the 'dream palaces', transformed the entire cinema-going experience for the audience. It wasn't just the larger seating capacity, these were awesomely grand places of entertainment with marble stairways, built in an over-the-top lavishly theatrical style. Some were decorated to look like an exotic tropical island, or in the style of an Indian maharaja's palace, or to resemble a Mediterranean resort.

Many were plush, Art Deco-style picture houses, often influenced by the architecture of Ancient Egypt, with huge screens, cigarette girls, even uniformed page boys. Some of the new palaces had smart cafés and tea rooms attached; the highlight of many featured the imported Wurlitzer organ, brightly lit and rising up from the floor, complete with organist to entertain the audience during the interval. Audiences could wallow in total luxury and fantasy – reflecting the dream world of movies – for just a few pennies a seat.

The dream palaces tended to flourish most of all in the poorer areas where a warm, comfortable environment was virtually unknown. Many in the audience were actually walking on carpet for the first time. Some opted to indulge in the sheer escapism of the dream palace for an entire afternoon and evening, watching the programme continuously.

There were usually two films in each programme with newsreels like Pathé News and trailers in between. Newsreels had been around in cinemas since the era of silent film but became prominent in the mid-1930s: some city centres boasted small newsreel cinemas showing nothing else. Only with the arrival of TV in homes in the 1950s did the newsreels begin to disappear.

The programmes mainly featured American films. British films were shown too, though the homegrown films, produced to a quota system, tended to be much less popular with audiences, relegated to 'B'-movie status (the bottom half of a double feature).

Youngsters frequently packed out the stalls in the dream palaces. The stalls were the cheapest seats (6 pence), the upstairs seats, slightly more expensive (9 pence), especially if 'U' certificate films (which under-sixteens could watch without being accompanied by an adult) were showing.

Saturday clubs specially for children took hold in the 1930s and continued through and beyond the war years. Nicknamed the 'Tuppenny Rush', the children's programme consisted of a cartoon, followed by a sixty-minute B-movie Western, plus a ten-minute episode of a twelve-part serial, ending with a 'cliffhanger'. The kids would sit cheering their heroes or jeering loudly at the bad guys. Usherettes and cinema managers often had their work cut out to prevent youngsters from jumping all over the seats, or having to catch naughty non-payers craftily creeping in through the emergency exits.

Animated cartoon characters like Mickey Mouse became hugely popular with audiences by the mid-1930s, but it was Walt Disney's first ever animated music fantasy film, *Snow White and the Seven Dwarfs*, that turned out to be a mega hit with UK cinema audiences in 1937, when one-third of the country went to see it.

Other box-office sensations in the months immediately after war was declared were the American Civil War epic, *Gone with the Wind*, starring Clark Gable and Vivien Leigh, and the Judy Garland classic, *The Wizard of Oz*. British-made films quickly tended towards somewhat obvious propaganda yet they became popular too; a film called *The Lion Has Wings*, made by celebrated filmmaker Alexander Korda, focused on the superiority of the RAF. It became one of the top three box-office attractions of 1939.

Joyce Storey (see previous chapter) became a regular at 'the flicks' in the 1920s long before she left school.

If you were lucky, you could get into the first few rows of the sevenpences, which came halfway up the hall and just right to be able to see the silver screen without cricking your neck. Right next to the cinema was a sweet shop with bottles of sweets and an array of mouth-watering chocolates for sixpence a quarter.

Courting couples usually got the chocs and they always sat in the balcony seats. Of course, this luxury depended on whether you were lucky enough to be going out with a young man who was in work, otherwise the pictures were right out and a walk round the park would have to suffice.

Everybody who could afford it went to the pictures every week. The kids went on Saturday afternoon. This cost us three whole pennies and was our pocket money for the week. *Ben-Hur* [1925] had been blazoned on the bill posters for weeks. With a cast of thousands, it was supposed to be sensational and special sound effects had been acquired at great expense.

Although the talkies were about to arrive in the late 1920s, the silent films were still with us and those who couldn't read the captions often had plenty of people around them to supply the story they missed. There would be long sighs and cries of 'Aah' when the villain of the piece did his dirty deeds, and as the film was projected onto the screen, the beam poured down through a thick haze of pipe and cigarette smoke that we coughed and spluttered through in order to see our favourite actors appear on the screen.'

Janet Gaynor, Charles Farrell, Fredric March, Douglas Fairbanks and Norma Shearer were just a few of these.

ENTERTAINMENT

They took us into another world of glamour and romance, and escape from the harsh, drab reality of our lives. As schoolgirls, we copied the women's hairstyles and tried to emulate them. The false became the real.

But no film could start before the pianist arrived. He was the most important man in those far-off days of silent movies. When he arrived at the cinema and began to walk down the red-carpeted aisle, applause, whistling and foot-stamping would accompany him all the way down to the cinema pit, where his grand piano always stood. It was his inspired playing that could bring a lump to your throat when our hero was nigh unto death and our heroine ministered to him, or fill you with fear and trepidation when Indians charged the stagecoach, or prompt you to rise in your seat to urge the hero to sock the villain to death, or kick his teeth in, and to boo and shout until you were hoarse.

Then the talking pictures arrived.

They built a new cinema just down the road and my friend Vee and I screamed and held onto each other when the pale horse of death seemed to leap out of the screen and onto us. Everything was now larger than life and full of energy and movement. We raced down to the new cinema before school one morning to gaze at a large poster outside showing Carlotta King dancing in a flame-coloured dress and John Bowles in flowing Arab headgear from the [silent] film *The Desert Song*. We gazed in rapt attention then turned and ran all the way to the school gates with the bell ringing madly in our ears. Out of breath and just making it to school in time, we whispered to each other as we filed into class that we would go on Friday night, because Saturday would be so crowded, we might have to queue for hours.

Friday, we could go straight from school as long as we let our parents know. We could take sandwiches and call on a couple of mates who lived down that way and then we would be ready to be first in the queue for the evening performance.

As an eight-year-old in North London, Terry Gallacher (1929–2014) developed a passion for cinema that eventually led to a lifetime's career in film and TV, first as a newsreel cameraman, then a TV news editor and eventually running his own post-production company. It all started in 1937.

My principal visits to the cinema were on a Saturday morning. Around eight o'clock in the morning, I would approach my mother for some pocket money. She might give me two pennies, sometimes three; my dad would give me the same. On a bad week, I would have as little as threepence in total. Then I would go up to my granddad's room and ask him if he had any money for me to go to the pictures. He would ask me to pass him his small terracotta jar, with a lid. From here, he took out some farthings and he would count out four [totalling one penny]. I had to have fourpence to get into the Moorish-styled cinema, the

Alcazar, in Edmonton, which started at nine in the morning and ran until midday. Here, we would see a couple of B movies about kids and animals and then a large number of serials like *Tailspin Tommy*, *The Perils of Pauline*, *Flash Gordon* and films like *Tarzan* with Johnny Weissmuller.

Of course, they were all designed to get us back there next week. Mostly these cliffhangers were cheating us. *Tailspin Tommy* would be plunging to earth in a dive that he could not possibly pull out of. Next week, he would be seen about a hundred foot higher and pulls out of the dive without a problem.

The audience were exclusively children, no adults were allowed. Most of the children were restless and rowdy. Frequently, the noise of the audience would be greater than the characters on screen. At this point, the resident warder would march down the aisle, shouting, 'Quack, Quack!' With my fourpenny ticket I could sit in the circle, far away from the rabble below. They were so bad, fights among the roughest of them were not unknown. If I could not have got fourpence to sit in the circle, I would not go. It took me a long time to work out that the warder was shouting 'Quiet!' It really did sound like 'Quack!'

If I had a good day and rustled up another twopence, I could join the 'Tuppenny Rush' at the Hippodrome across the road. The management of the Hippodrome, early experts in marketing, arranged to open their performance thirty minutes after the show ended at the Alcazar. All those children, trying to go from the Alcazar to the Hippodrome, would evacuate the former at high speed, run down to the crossing, over the road and queue up outside the Hippodrome. Traffic was held up while this mob moved from one cinema to the next. The main reason for the rush was that the Hippodrome only held half as many as the Alcazar and you couldn't risk the chance that more wanted to go to the Hippodrome than it could hold.

In the Hip, the films were older; the rowdiest of the Alcazar audience were sure to attend (their parents probably suffered considerable hardship raising the extra twopence, just to get rid of them for a few more hours); there were broken seats, seats with the most outrageous mixtures of spilled food, forcing us to inspect each seat before sitting down.

The projector frequently broke down, the audience would go wild. They would shout, 'Ooh, ooh, ooh' until the picture came back. Here there was no refuge sitting in a circle – there wasn't one – and there was no 'Quack' man. In the Hippodrome, there was only the occasional cry of pain as a rowdy became the recipient of a thick ear.

The warder in the Hippodrome was silent but quite active. I don't know why I went there.

Sadly, the Alcazar was bombed in a very early wartime raid on North London on 23 August 1940, while the Hip was pulled down – much to the relief of the local populace.

'IT'LL NEVER CATCH ON'

Cinema had only one other competing form of mass entertainment: radio. Television was barely in its infancy in the pre-war years. Very early TV sets demonstrating pictures with sound were seen by the public at London's Earl's Court Exhibition Centre in the summer of 1936 but given the tiny screens with flickering black-and-white images and the outrageously high price of a set – somewhere between £50 and £125 (at a time when average earnings for a year were just £132) – it seemed unlikely that TV would ever take over from the radio as the number one form of home entertainment. (There were 20,000 working TV sets in London when war broke out – only for the service to be abruptly terminated in September 1939, in the midst of a Mickey Mouse cartoon, resuming again in 1946.)

By the late 1920s, 'wireless' – as radio was known then – was in its infancy, but it was growing incredibly fast. Kits for home construction of a radio set were widely advertised and became hugely popular. London-based electronics firms like Lissen and A. C. Cossor Ltd were at the forefront of radio development in the UK, initially selling kits to enthusiastic amateurs wanting to build a DIY version of a radio set on their kitchen table.

These kit sets, complete with three valves, a cabinet and speaker, were advertised at prices ranging from £11 10s to a more modest £6 5s in 1934. Given the high price, radio enthusiasts were offered 'Convenient gradual payment terms' (a punishing early form of credit or 'never-never' with high interest rates: repossession would follow after just a couple of missed payments). A fast-growing publishing industry also cashed in on the growing radio craze with specialist magazines for enthusiasts.

But the days of wireless sets with accumulator batteries that were only rechargeable at a garage were dying. By the mid-1930s, mass production of small home radios by firms like Lissen and A. C. Cossor meant prices for a working set gradually went down: a brand-new radio could now be purchased for £5 and 5 shillings.

By 1937, over half of UK households had a radio. Two years later, nearly nine million 10-shilling radio licences were taken out. These were the first broadcast licences, a forerunner of today's TV licence. Broadcast licences were first issued in 1922, when the BBC began radio transmission.

RADIO DAYS

Don Carter was the youngest of ten, born in 1920. He grew up in the Tenantry Down area of East Sussex. As a schoolboy, he would listen to a very early radio set in the home he shared with his widowed father and siblings.

The first radios were known as wireless sets. Heaven knows why, they were all wires. The very first were known as crystal sets and reception was obtained by what was known as a 'cat's whisker', which was moved around by means of a lever in close proximity to the crystal.

The first wireless we had required an aerial running the full length of the garden from a height of fifteen or twenty feet, like a high clothes line. It also needed a copper rod buried in the ground as an earth. The set itself was an upturned wooden box on top of which were several valves of different kinds [transistors had not then been invented, they did not become available until the late 1950s]. One of these valves lit up. There were two coils which could be moved closer together or further apart, as required. There were one or two more bits and pieces – beyond my comprehension – and two enormous tuning dials about the size of a large teacup and an 'on' and 'off' switch on the front of the box.

Under the box, there was a tangle of wires connecting all the parts together. At this time I do not think there were any wireless sets connected to the electrical mains. Batteries and accumulators provided the power (in our home there was no electricity). The amount of power that had to be supplied by the batteries was something in the order of 120 volts. There were no 120-volt batteries at that time. However, there was a flat torch battery from which protruded two metal tags, the positive and negative poles. They provided a current of 4.5 volts. A sufficient number of such batteries had to be connected together by brass clips to provide the equivalent power. The accumulator had to be taken to the local wireless shop for recharging about once a fortnight, this cost just a few coppers [pennies]. As this process took a couple of days, it was advisable to have a spare accumulator. This was for a wireless set that was only used in the evenings.

There was no loudspeaker, just one pair of earphones. How then did the family listen in? The earphones were placed in a china pudding basin and the resulting resonance was somehow supposed to improve sound quality.

Reception was extremely poor by today's standards. There were all kinds of atmospheric interferences, whistles, crackles, long whooping sounds. It was as if we were trying to make contact with outer space. Despite all this, it still seemed worthwhile to rush home from school to book a place next to the pudding basin. After all, not many of your schoolmates had such a contrivance. We would probably not have had one if it had not been for the fact that one of my brothers, who was an electrician, had a workmate who was very interested in the subject.

Wireless was definitely the up-and-coming thing then. It seemed that every young man was busy building his own set.

What were those early radio audiences listening to? The first ever BBC radio broadcast came in November 1922. Most programmes were broadcast live, a mixture of music, talks, news and weather forecasts. There was *Children's Hour* from 5–6pm; news itself was only broadcast after 6pm. Live sporting events were broadcast, but no sporting results were given out. Incredibly, newsreaders in the studio would read the news of the day in evening dress, speaking in posh, Oxford-type accents.

Sunday listening was limited. There were no radio broadcasts on Sunday morning or early evening (since so many people went to church each Sunday, it was feared broadcasts might discourage this).

By the 1930s, radio light entertainment mostly focused on dance band shows until the first ever radio comedy show, merging comedy with music, started in 1938. This was Wednesday night's *Band Waggon* with Arthur Askey and Richard Murdoch, Audiences loved it. In fact, it became so popular that cinema managers complained that their box-office receipts plummeted every Wednesday night. The show ran until 1940, but ended when Murdoch went into the RAF and Askey left to pursue a hugely successful career in film and TV, which incuded sitcoms.

When war broke out, the BBC closed down all regional stations; all programmes were from the BBC Home Service. Radio, by this time, especially news, music and comedy, had become a crucial element in the life of the nation – as it proved to be throughout the war.

Along with a trip to the cinema, a once-weekly outing to a dance venue played a huge part in people's social lives. Throughout the 1930s the dance-hall boom spread right across the country as the popularity of dancing grew. It was estimated that Glasgow, for instance, had more dance halls per head of population than anywhere else in the country.

The dance hall, village hop or church social were frequently the places where the majority of couples first met. Dancing was one of the very few activities that parents of unmarried girls deemed 'respectable' enough to allow a girl to go off with a group of friends for a night out at a local palais. Unmarried women then were, by today's standards, extremely limited in what they could do unaccompanied. Public houses or cocktail bars, for instance, were completely off-limits for single women on their own; only women of dubious reputation would venture inside unaccompanied.

As with the movies, the weekly dancing habit escalated during the war, especially in the big city dance venues, when around 10,000 people a week would pack into huge halls, some of which ran four separate sessions a day.

Dancing was a great morale booster. Servicemen and women with just a few hours' leave, as well as local habitués, would gravitate onto the floor to perform the more traditional dances like the tango, the foxtrot or the waltz, or the livelier conga, rumba or hokey cokey.

Frank Mee (see Chapter 4), from Stockton-on Tees, was born in February 1929. He still has vivid memories of the dance floor, from the late 1930s onwards.

In the larger dance halls, you danced on sprung floors or at least highly polished and prepared floors. In small halls, it was plank floors with nails sticking up or on concrete with linoleum squares glued down.

Any kind of footwear would do, but some people had dancing pumps and others wore what they had down to hobnail boots – frowned upon if it was a polished floor.

I lived for dancing, young as I was. Dad said I would have danced on the pigsty roof, if he had played the music

– too true! Where most lads saw dancing as a means to an end, i.e. girls, for me dancing *was* the end, the girls were the means.

At ten, I had been given an insight into the wonder and splendour of the dance hall. My parents were competition dancers at a time when money or gifts could be won. They had different partners for the competitions and we had a house full of prizes of various kinds they had won.

As the babysitter was loath to look after me (I was a bit of a handful, she said), I was dressed up and taken to the local Co-op (Co-op Dance Halls were to be found all over the country). I would sit quietly and take it all in, overawed by the combined beauty of the music, lights and swirling dancers in the multi-coloured flowing dresses. The men wore sober suits or tuxedos. All my life I never failed to be amazed at the splendour and ambience of those large dance halls.

The high, often domed ceiling had masses of spotlights that changed colour as they turned. The huge mirrored ball, with the spotlight on each corner of the room shining on it as it turned, cast scattered beams of moonlight on the dancers as the main lights dimmed to a soft haze. The coloured spotlights would weave among the dancers, wrapping them in a warm, ethereal glow as it passed – it was wonder indeed.

Most halls had plush settees along the walls, with a scattering of tables and chairs. One end would be a standing area and the other end taken up by the stage. We had some large dance bands in some of those dance halls. The players would come on stage in their tuxedos and the band leader would stand up front. He waved his arms, did his little dance steps and sang the odd song, smiling all the while at the ladies passing.

During those early days of watching, I was often taken on the floor by ladies during the interval between competitions. I was quite tall and a quick learner, so I could soon do most of the old-fashioned dances, as they were called. In the interval, records would be played of the modern dances, so I got a feeling for the quickstep, waltz and foxtrot – an early learning curve without a doubt.

By the time I was in high school, we were dancing three or four times a week in church halls, school halls, and I was going to Cochran's Dance Studio for lessons in modern dancing. The vicar or church workers would run the church hall dances, mainly to a record player or on occasion a three-piece band. We got a night of Victor Sylvester records, one of the UK's most successful musicians and bandleaders of the ballroom dancing era, though us scallywags would try to sneak a Glenn Miller onto the machine [Miller was an American big-band trombonist, bandleader and composer of the Swing era; musically, one of the most popular dance sounds of the Second World War until his tragic death in a plane crash in 1944].

We had to do a duty dance with the vicar's wife and the tea ladies as behoves young gentlemen. One local spinster of undecided age took a shine to me and would come dashing over. She would wrap me in a wrestling hold from which there was no escape, pull me to her bosom and then do a sort of military two-step to whatever dance was being played. My memory is of an overwhelming smell of mothballs wafting round my nose. It ended all lascivious thoughts right there – the smell of mothballs was a passion killer all my life. I did get a tea and bun paid for, so stood the punishment. Another memory is of dancing with an older woman. She was the spitting image of Carmen Miranda, the film star. She'd take me on the floor for the tango or rumba, pull me in tight and say, 'Touch my bones, feel the movement.' She was right and I soon stopped blushing beetroot red.

Throughout my life, dancing got me new friends, wherever I was. I danced in many of the largest halls in the country and loved every minute of it. Many of us met our partners in dance halls. I eventually met my late wife of sixty years at a dance. She was also a good dancer and we did English-style demonstrations when we went abroad, by request.

Dancing and cinema aside, there were other pervasive influences at play in the late 1930s, especially for women. There was nothing new in magazines for them, but by the mid-1930s, new printing technology offered a far more tempting read. High-circulation magazines like *Woman's Own* and *Woman* were launched in 1932 and 1937, respectively, with *Woman* quickly establishing itself as the market leader, selling one million copies a week by the time war broke out. The formula was a standard combination of romantic fiction, health and beauty, knitting patterns, dressmaking, gardening, cookery and household management, but the inclusion of photos and articles about the most glamorous, if remote, influencers of the era, the Royal Family and the big Hollywood movie stars of the time, proved to be the main circulation booster. Home and hearth with a dash of glitter!

As for the Royal Family, their overall popularity did not wane, despite the bad 1920s years of the Depression, unemployment and hunger marches. Big celebrations for the Silver Jubilee of King George V in May 1935 gave the people the opportunity to celebrate and show their love of King and Country.

It was a big day for patriotism. The King himself was reported to have commented that he had never seen so many people on the streets. London's centre was lit up by floodlights, flags and bunting festooned the streets everywhere and the nation celebrated the public holiday with sporting events, pageants and street parties. Frank Mee recalled:

We got a day off school and as was usual, the Green at Norton became the playground for the crowds having a day out from the town, a tuppenny bus ride away. We got a bag of buns from the local bakery and a Jubilee mug. The day off school was the main thing for me – freedom! Our local board school was very old and dreary to someone like me, used to a large garden-cum-smallholding to play in.

A year later, King George V was dead and we were

celebrating Edward VIII. My parents had many discussions about him and Mrs Simpson [Wallis Simpson, the American divorcée with whom the soon-to-be King was in love].

I gathered there was a lot of antagonism around it all when he came to the throne in 1936. My parents definitely did not approve. We got another day off school, more buns and a new mug. The Green once again was a place of meeting, fun and games, with small stalls, roundabouts and Wall's Ice Cream ('Stop me and buy one') three-wheeled bicycles.

The new King's coronation was set for May 1937, but in December 1936, the King made a dramatic broadcast to the nation to inform them that he was abdicating the throne for the twice-divorced American, Wallis Simpson.

The public knew little of the story of the relationship, but what they did hear met with much disapproval – exactly like the views of Frank Mee's parents.

Foreign newspapers had widely reported the relationship with Mrs Simpson – but such was the scandal of the relationship at the time, the British people had been more or less kept in the dark, partly because of official restraints on news coverage. As the dashing Prince of Wales, Edward had been extremely popular. Now he was gone, more or less in permanent exile in France with his new wife and a new title: the Duke of Windsor.

His brother Albert, known as Bertie, his wife Elizabeth and their two daughters, Elizabeth (the present Queen, Elizabeth II) and her sister Margaret, were catapulted, overnight, into a life they had never really anticipated, following Bertie's coronation as George VI in May 1937.

It was a startlingly dramatic beginning, but by the end of 1937, the new Royal Family were established in Buckingham Palace and despite the King's stammer and consequent dislike of speaking in public, Bertie, Elizabeth and their daughters were destined to prove even more popular than George V and his wife, Queen Mary.

The then Princess Elizabeth drew much admiration round the world when, aged fourteen, she made a radio address to evacuated children in October 1940, during the Battle of Britain. The war years helped to cement the people's love for their Royal Family – Britain was still very much a patriotic nation.

A FITTER NATION

Attitudes to fitness took a leap forward in the 1930s. The background to this had been the toll that poor nutrition and living standards had taken on many male volunteers during the First World War, making them unfit for military service.

Today's fitness obsession had its early roots back in 1930, when the Women's League of Health and Beauty was formed by Mollie Bagot Stack, with the aim of making co-ordinated exercise available to all ages through dance, exercise and callisthenics (gymnastic exercises), the first ever concerted attempt to encourage people to view the regular group workout as a means of staying fit and healthy.

Membership was 2 shillings and 6 pence, classes cost 6 pence and there was an affordable uniform of a white satin blouse and black satin knickers. Within seven years, the League had 160,000 members. It was cheap to join, and big displays of synchronised exercise were staged in London's Hyde Park and the Albert Hall, all heavily featured in the newsreels of the day.

Alongside this were other factors involving greater awareness of a healthy lifestyle. The growing Boy Scout and Girl Guide movement, with its emphasis on outdoor life, was claiming membership of over one million by the end of the 1920s. Rambling or hiking in the country became a growing leisure activity, leading to the formation of the Ramblers' Association in 1935.

Outdoor swimming was also rapidly developing as a healthy pursuit. To this end, from the mid-1930s local councils in seaside resorts invested heavily in new swimming pool lidos, since having a public swimming pool was then viewed as being as important as it had been to offer visitors a pier half a century before.

A total of 169 new lidos were built across the UK by local authorities during the 1930s, both for seaside holidaymakers and city dwellers. By the late 1930s, Londoners could enjoy huge newly built open-air lidos in Chingford, Tottenham, Edmonton and Brockwell; in the north of England, Morecambe's Super Swimming Stadium, opened in July 1936, was reputed at the time to be Europe's largest outdoor pool.

The need for Britain to focus on health and fitness was reinforced by the country's poor performance at the Berlin Olympics in August 1936, which the Nazis used to promote an image of a new, strong, united Germany, with the emphasis on physical fitness, masking the reality of their aims as a racist and increasingly violent regime. But the message from the imagery of the Olympics was clear: a physically fit younger generation would make a more formidable fighting force in wartime.

The following year, the British government launched the National Fitness Council, with the aim of launching a nationwide keep-fit campaign. Local authorities were encouraged to make land available for improving sporting and outdoor activities. By then, of course, war was moving onto the horizon.

Yet even as plans were being drawn up for food rationing and how the nation could be fed in wartime, the 1930s phenomenon of health and fitness – and the significance of diet – came into play. It meant that new discoveries about nutrition could play an important part in feeding the nation, despite wartime shortages.

The wartime food rationing diet that was drawn up for the nation, spartan as it was, was basically nutritious. It had been carefully calculated by scientists and statisticians. Rationing also forced people to adopt new eating patterns so that those who had previously consumed a poor diet could increase their intake of protein and vitamins, since everyone received the same ration. As a result, many people had a better diet under wartime food rationing than before the war years, with a consequent improvement in the nation's health.

Moreover, the keep-fit craze of the 1930s continued to thrive post-war. By the 1950s, a popular keep-fit guru had emerged. Her name was Eileen Fowler, a fitness instructor who had toured the country during the war, conducting group physical training. She had a following of half a million BBC radio listeners regularly exercising to her programme at 6.45am each morning; the country's first ever keep-fit broadcasts. Fowler's career as a fitness expert would span radio and TV through the years: 'My aim in life is to keep families fit,' she declared. She died, aged ninety-three, in 2000.

8

HOLIDAYS

HOLIDAYS WITH PAY WERE VIRTUALLY UNKNOWN BEFORE THE First World War. Even in 1925, just one and a half million people were entitled to a paid holiday. That figure increased in 1937 (to four million) – still a tiny proportion, given that the workforce at the time was close to twenty million.

A Holidays with Pay Act introduced by the government in 1938 for industrial workers signalled change ahead – yet it was not enacted until after the war. Only then did paid holidays start to become more commonplace in the UK.

So, what sort of holidays would people take in the 1930s?

Holidays abroad were not on the agenda. Those were strictly for the rich and privileged. Flying was relatively new, though the general public were well aware of the enormous travel possibilities aviation opened up, thanks to cinema newsreels and newspaper stories about the exploits of aviators, especially homegrown flying heroines like Hull-born Amy Johnson, who stepped into global superstar status with her solo flight to Australia in 1930. Flying circuses, air displays at which anyone could queue up and pay for a short flight, also developed in the 1930s, increasing public awareness of aviation.

During the 1930s, commercial aviation expanded. Passenger flights were available, albeit at a price that was far too expensive for most – and often very uncomfortable by today's standards. As for all-in affordable package holidays abroad, inclusive of flight and hotel, these would not reach the budget of ordinary people until the late 1950s.

It had, of course, been the advent of the motor car right at the beginning of the twentieth century that altered the pattern of life generally. Car ownership in the 1930s was still very low by modern standards – a total of just under two million privately owned vehicles were on the road in 1938 – but there were also close to half a million motorbikes, many with sidecars, as well as large numbers of scheduled bus and coach services on the roads. And, of course, trains were an easy means of transport to seaside resort or countryside.

Going to the coast or the seaside, of course, had been an established leisure activity as far back as the beginning of the railways in the mid-1800s, which ushered in the development of well over a hundred seaside resort towns in Britain by the end of the nineteenth century.

Around that time, a tradition of an unpaid one-week summer holiday for workers was established. At first, it was the Lancashire cotton-mill owners who enabled this, closing their factories for a week – and in turn, all shops, post offices and schools in the area closed too.

Known as Wakes Week, this one-week factory closure tradition spread to other industrial towns in Yorkshire, Staffordshire and other parts of the Midlands, where from mid-July to mid-September, each town closed down to enable workers to enjoy a week or two's holiday at a big, bustling seaside resort like Blackpool, dubbed 'the pleasure factory' by the throngs of holidaymakers from Lancashire mill towns who holidayed there, or Morecambe, which attracted more visitors from Yorkshire and Scotland, thanks to its rail connections.

Further south, popular seaside resorts like Eastbourne, Brighton, Worthing, Bognor and Bournemouth, with their attractive piers, promenades and pretty beach huts, were also drawing more and more summer holidaymakers and day-trippers, though such were the social distinctions of the times, certain summer resorts held themselves aloof in order to lure a better class of visitor.

Snooty Eastbourne, in East Sussex, – 'built by gentlemen for gentlemen' – banned slot machines on its pier. Frinton-on-Sea, Essex, took great pains to distinguish itself from its brasher neighbour, Clacton-on-Sea – known as 'the town of temperance' Frinton did not have a single pub until the year 2000 and ice cream vendors were banned from the beach. Bexhill, also in East Sussex, which still boasts one of the 1930s most iconic leisure centres – the Art Deco De La Warr Pavilion – saw itself as infinitely more genteel, its visitors vastly superior to the crowds of 'Kiss Me Quick'-hatted day-trippers in neighbouring Hastings. And so on. Seaside snobbery prevailed in the 1920s and 1930s, but it couldn't stop millions enjoying what Britain's coastline had to offer.

FAMILY TIME

Frank Mee's childhood holidays in the 1930s were journeys by car to coastal resorts or beauty spots near his home in Stockton-on-Tees, County Durham.

Holidays were a regular thing for my sister Sylvia and I. My father had two cars, a newish Ford 8 and an Austin 7 two-seater with two dicky seats [fold-out seats at the back of the car, where the boot would usually be]. We would pile in the Ford, Sylvia and I, our two cousins, Timmy and Jeffrey, Mum, Dad driving, Aunt Phyllis and Uncle Cecil, complete with picnic. Often a freshly cooked pie and cakes, fresh-baked bread, our own ham and salad, plus tea maker, a paraffin stove thing, cups, plates and crockery, then off to the coast. We went to Seaton Carew [a small seaside resort in Hartlepool] one way or Redcar Marske or Saltburn, the other way. Sometimes it would be the Cleveland Hills or the Moors, the Sheepwash [on the North Yorkshire Moors] being a favourite.

I blotted my copybook with Aunt Phyllis, who was not called 'The Princess' for nothing – she dressed for every occasion. One time, I was sitting between her and Uncle Cecil, with a bilberry pie on my knee. When we got to Marske, there was a rush to get out to play. I put the pie on the seat Cecil had been on. Aunt Phyllis, dressed in a fashionable white suit, getting out of the car, fell back on the pie. White and bilberry definitely do not mix! She made Dad drive her back home to change and came back dressed more for the ballroom than the beach – I was never forgiven.

Dad would also take Mother, Sylvia and I to Saltburn-by-the-Sea, where we would stay in a boarding house for a week. He went home to continue to work while we had a very enjoyable time on the beach, rockpool diving or sitting in the Italian Gardens, listening to bands play. We also had relatives in Goathland [a North Yorkshire village in the Scarborough area, the setting for the TV series *Heartbeat*]. They were sheep farmers. Sylvia and I would often spend a week's holiday with them.

Our relatives would all come to stay with us when it was Stockton Horse Racing Week. The women all went shopping in Stockton's famous market – the widest High Street in the country, so it was said. The men went to the races and then the pub later.

My piano got a good thrashing when they were all here, as singing round the piano was what we did. After a couple of nights, they were back on the trains and gone. Dad then got the piano retuned for my practice.

Caravanning holidays also started to proliferate in the 1930s as motoring became more popular. The earliest versions designed to be pulled by a motor car were produced by Eccles Motor Transport in Birmingham. This early type of Eccles caravan was essentially a box on wheels; later models in the 1920s were incredibly heavy to tow, made of wood, lined with hard woods like mahogany and with cupboards made of oak.

By the early 1930s, the squarer original designs gave way to more streamlined models and by the end of the decade, caravans were larger, with baths under the floor, toilet compartments, gas cooking facilities and built-in radios.

Caravanners tended to be prosperous – a four-berth Eccles caravan sold for £130 in the mid-1930s – and celebrities of the day, like Gracie Fields, were deployed to help promote the attractions of caravanning. The fast-growing Caravan Club of Great Britain started to hold rallies in the early 1930s, requiring members to turn up for dances in full evening dress. Caravan parks were virtually non-existent in the pre-war years: people could park by the road or in a field at night (after the war ended, such was the severe housing shortage, many caravans were lived in full time).

Hiking and rambling were other outdoor pursuits for the health-minded holidaymaker. By the early 1930s, the rambling boom soon gave way to other holidaymaking activities, like youth hostelling, cycling and camping.

For families on a tight budget, pitching a tent in a field was an affordable, if somewhat basic, way of holidaying. It became so popular through the decade that new laws banning the sales of milk, bread and butter on campsites were introduced amid government concern: it was felt that the countryside was at risk of being swamped by poor people.

D. A. Bishop remembers his early camping holidays in the late 1920s and 1930s:

My holidays might have been on a fairly primitive level but they were really enjoyable nonetheless. At our Methodist church in Plumstead, South-East London, we got to know of a camping club set up by a nearby sister church and it wasn't long before some of us youngsters were invited to join. In those early days the holidaymakers were almost all children or teenagers, but during the 1930s the inclusion of family tents was adopted, after which my mother would also take my two younger siblings. Dad went only once, but then he usually volunteered to supervise school journeys and never seemed keen on the idea of family holidays anyway.

My first experience of the Invicta Camping Club was when the chosen site was Pagham, just outside Bognor Regis, West Sussex. This resort had just earned the Royal title after King George V had recuperated there in 1929 after a serious illness. Aged thirteen at the time and despite prevailing unsettled weather, I thoroughly enjoyed being able to holiday with so many young people. Our homes for the fortnightly summer breaks were ex-army bell tents, comfortable enough under most conditions, although it paid to be able to select a really sound one.

Unlike modern tented homes, any facilities consisted of whatever we could provide that would fit into our very limited space. The only provided extra was a straw-stuffed palliasse [mattress]. An advance party would travel down on the Friday afternoon to set up tents and fill the palliasses and a large marquee housing a 'honky-tonk' piano would be erected by professionals.

After the inclusion of family camping and when our church had become more fully integrated, the catering was taken over by a volunteer couple from our church, who did a marvellous job with the limited funds available. The usual charge for the two-week holiday did not exceed £2 at the time.

Our very able pair generously augmented the kitty by adding their Co-op dividend for their own purchases during the year and I well recall how the menus satisfied even the voracious appetites of myself and friends.

The appetising smell of good bacon being cooked over an open fire was usually enough to ensure prompt attendance at breakfast by even the laziest members, who would otherwise be suffering by lunchtime. Bread and butter with marmalade taken from 7-pound stone jars completed the meal, for which unlimited tea would be available from a huge urn.

The camp's only paid member, who was keen enough to work very hard for his pittance, was known as Old Cookie. Of indeterminate age but definitely elderly, he cheerfully supervised cooking during the whole two weeks, usually being pressed to take a solitary half-day out of camp.

Our own fatigues would be limited to an hour or so each week, with perhaps an occasional forage for firewood. In-camp entertainment would be laid on at least once a week to include all local talent. For some of that we knew we could rely on Old Cookie, who would have regaled us for far too long, given full rein. His star piece song bore the title 'She 'It Me Wiv A Poker', a gory little number providing an insight into domestic disharmony during the late-Victorian period.

In later years, when our camping sites included Somerset, Devon and Dorset, our style became rather more sophisticated when some of us were able to take our own cars. On my earliest venture I remember a spirited discussion as to whether the old motor coach would manage to reach the summit of Berry Hill before running down towards Bognor.

Inevitably, juvenile romances were set up, but for my own part in those days, I was content to enjoy the romance of the English countryside and seaside.

Two scenes which have remained vivid in my memory: viewing Corfe Castle in Dorset by the light of a full moon on a wonderful summer night, and taking in the grandeur of Fingle Bridge in Dartmoor (the latter is part of the upper

Teign Gorge as the wild river flows rapidly towards the sea on the South Devon coast).

Without the discovery of the Invicta Camping Club, my early life would have been very much poorer.

By the mid-1930s, the wind of change was blowing. The typical British holidaymaking experience had distinct shortcomings sometimes, given the combination of the unreliability of the climate and the system of inexpensive bed and breakfasts run by landladies who did not want guests to linger on the premises until the evening meal. The idea of a very large holiday camp, where families on a budget could be accommodated, fed and entertained round the clock, all for one price, might have seemed ambitious at the outset. Yet this idea – an obvious gap in the market – would transform Britain's leisure industry, thanks to a man called Billy (later Sir William) Butlin.

The first ever Butlin's holiday camp opened its doors at Skegness, Lincolnshire, at Easter 1936, officially opened by its guest of honour, the aviatrix Amy Johnson. The brainchild of the entrepreneurial Butlin, a showman with a background in running hoop-la stalls and managing seaside amusement parks, the first Butlin's cost £100,000 to build and could accommodate 1,000 people.

A Butlin's Camp was effectively a miniature seaside resort with the focus on giving holidaymakers a chance to escape from everyday life. The overall style of building was modern in appearance, and there would be an outdoor swimming pool with cascades. Inside, there were large dining rooms, bars in the style of a grand hotel or luxury liner and ballrooms, all designed to create an atmosphere of luxury. The chalets where the campers slept were up-to-date for the times, with hot and cold running water, but these were built in a traditional, more homely mock-Tudor style with exposed beams.

Entertainment was at the heart of the Butlin's holiday camp experience, with the company's famous Redcoats on hand to ensure that everyone, of all ages, had a good time. By the standards of the day, it was a good deal: a week's full board, with three meals a day and free entertainment for all, for £3 a week at peak season. Promoted by Butlin as 'A week's holiday for a week's wage', it was a revolutionary idea whose time had come, though the majority of early Butlin's campers tended to be lower middle class, like bank clerks and their wives.

A second Butlin's, at Clacton-on-Sea in Essex, followed in 1938. A third Butlin's camp at Filey, North Yorkshire, which Billy Butlin planned to be the jewel in his crown, was half-finished when war broke out and the three camps were requisitioned as military bases.

After the war, more camps opened up and the Butlin's brand became one of the country's most successful and well-loved holiday venues. With the coming of the 1970s and the era of the cheap package holiday abroad, however, British holidaymaking habits changed. Subsequently, Butlin's was sold to the Rank Organisation in the 1970s, although the brand still lives on, with three Butlin's family resorts in Minehead, Bognor Regis and Skegness.

Bill Hathaway and his two brothers were Londoners with relatives in Skegness, on the Lincolnshire coast.

My uncle kept a wet-fish shop there, so during the holidays, my mother took us to stay before the Second World War. In the mornings, she worked as a cashier in the shop, where it was not considered hygienic for a shop assistant to handle notes and coins as well as the raw fish. We three boys were left to amuse ourselves.

Even in the early 1930s it was obvious that the sea was abandoning Skeggy. South Parade, the road that once fronted the sea, still had the eight-foot drop to what was once the beach, but now the sand had been replaced by lawns and gardens. Even further out was the vast boating lake and only beyond that did the beach begin.

Along the sea front ran the ancient charabancs with their bench seats stretching the width of the vehicles. It cost a penny to ride from the Clock Tower all the way to Uncle Arthur's, the amusement park opposite the Derbyshire Miners' Home at the north end of the sands. We didn't think Uncle Arthur's was a patch on Butlin's bigger, brighter amusement park back down the beach, seaward of the clock tower.

Butlin's Big Dipper was higher, faster and noisier than Uncle Arthur's and day and night, a clown, in coloured lights, bounced a ball – also in lights – across the front of the park.

HOLIDAYS

In those pre-war days, the sea still reached Skegness pier. Admission for children was a penny, though I remember one year, as an advertising gimmick, you could go on free by showing your Ovaltineys badge [Ovaltineys was the name of a 1930s children's club to promote the sale of Ovaltine, a sweet, malt-flavoured drink made with hot milk and often drunk as a nightcap].

There was another way on, much more exciting, during the year they were repairing the decking on the pier. By scrambling up the ironwork and along the supports over the sea, a boy could pop up through a hole in the planking halfway along – all free! On the pier were the penny-in-the-slot machines with such names as 'The Allwin' – which usually meant the 'All Lose' – and models in glass cases of things like prison buildings, where a penny would open the big doors to show a prisoner surrounded by officials, including the Governor and a parson. A figure of a warder moved a lever and the prisoner, with a noose around his neck, dropped through the trap-door, which opened beneath his feet. It was all over in a few seconds!

At the very end of the pier was a tall lattice tower with diving boards. At high tide times, Leslie, a man who had lost a hand in an accident, drew crowds by performing spectacular dives. His swallow dives, half- and full twists and back and front somersaults kept the spectators applauding as he climbed the ladder from the sea back to the top of his tower. He constantly reminded the audience that 'some of my young ladies will pass among you with a collecting box.

Don't forget the diver, every penny makes the water warmer.'

Along part of the boating lake was an artificial cliff. There was a passage through – 'The Axenstrasse' – with openings over the lake and a promenade at the top. This 'cliff' was one of my favourite climbs. Several years ago, to the embarrassment of my wife and the surprise of a couple walking along the top, I climbed it again. They didn't expect to see an old gentleman appear over the edge of the cliff, artificial or not.

Happy days! Good old Skeggy!

Rambling or hiking holidays were another popular, inexpensive option. Youth hostel accommodation was cheap – about 1 shilling a night – and some offered cooking facilities too. It was all very basic: segregated dorms, smoking or drinking banned, lights out at 10.30pm, but for the health-minded, the price was right. By 1939, Britain boasted close to three hundred youth hostels dotted around the country, many in remote or scenic locations.

Such was the craze for rambling or hiking that the railway companies, always keen to commercialise a trend, started offering an unusual type of excursion: the Mystery Hiking trip. One-day excursions out of mainline stations, like Paddington in London, were priced at a few shillings for a return train trip to an unknown destination.

Once on the train, passengers were handed maps and information on the 'secret' destination; the train drivers did not know their route until they opened a sealed envelope containing the information. On arrival, groups of passengers started their hike, following the maps with the prescribed route − which often included a meal along the way. A healthy day out with an element of surprise. Railway companies as far away as Australia and New Zealand quickly took note and also started selling these mystery train rides.

For most children, a summer holiday meant a stay with relatives.

Dawn[*] and her brother Eric spent most of the school summer holiday on the beach near their home in Whitley Bay, in Northumberland. One week every summer was spent with their grandparents, travelling by train or bus to visit them.

For Eric and me, that was either Bishop Auckland or Sedgefield [both in County Durham]. Sedgefield was very primitive, lit only by oil lamps, and water had to be drawn from the village pump and carried home in large white enamelled buckets. Rainwater was collected in barrels and used for washing facilities. Country food was too rich for me: fresh cream and butter, raw fruit straight from the garden, eggs still warm from the hen's nest.

Granny was a farmer's daughter and an excellent cook, but it was not what we were used to. Granny's meats were roast pheasant, partridge, jugged hare, pigeon pie and even rook pie [a traditional country staple] − which was mainly little bones. No one was allowed to know Granny's recipes. She made delicious cakes and biscuits, jams, chutneys, pickled walnuts and mushrooms, having learned her culinary skills at home on the farm. Her husband – our grandfather – was registrar of births deaths and marriages. His office was in their house at Sedgefield; he also travelled to the local villages, writing letters for illiterate people. He had a pony and trap for such journeys.

Back at home, the beach was only a short walk away and there was very little traffic on the roads so it was quite safe for us to walk down. Tram cars ran from North Shields ferry to Whitley Bay bandstand on the Links. We had plenty of free entertainment with pierrots [male French pantomime clowns, traditional seaside entertainers from the late nineteenth and early twentieth centuries, clad in distinctive black-and-white or loose baggy costumes, with pointy hats with pom-poms] who performed at the bandstand and also on a stage below the slope on the Central Lower Promenade.

They really were very good performers, comedians who also danced and sang. There was an area roped off, which had deckchairs where the audience paid to sit. Of course, we schoolchildren never had any money so when the clowns came around with their collecting boxes, we disappeared onto the beach!

There was also Uncle Jim with his team of Evangelists on the beach, who played hymns on an organ. At the bottom of the slope on the Central Promenade a one-legged former serviceman from the 1914–18 War built beautiful sandcastles. He used coloured powders and sprinkled the finished castles in reds, greens and blues. People put coins in a box for the poor ex-soldier. Sometimes stray dogs would run across his castle or high tides would wash away his beautiful work. I can picture him yet with his suntanned skin and his peg-leg, which sank into the sand with each step.

There were sandcastle competitions for us children, sponsored by local newsagents – we had to buy a comic paper to display on our effort. There were other attractions on the beach: donkey rides and shuggy boats [big double-seated swings that looked like boats, suspended on iron rods, pulled on a rope to go backwards and forwards]. All these had to be paid for, so we learned very early in life that all these attractions and the roundabouts in Spanish City [an early leisure centre in Whitley Bay, opened in 1910 as a smaller version of Blackpool's Pleasure Beach] were for visitors only, not for us locals. As a birthday treat, we were given pennies to have a donkey ride.

Summers have always been brief on the north-east coast so beach traders had to find other ways of making a living. The pierrots played in the pantomimes at the Newcastle theatres, but August Bank Holiday was carnival time when two male pierrots were crowned king and queen and rode in an open-topped vehicle decorated with paper flowers, streamers and balloons. The carnival parade was competitive, children decorated their cycles and wore fancy dress. The merchants who had horses groomed their charges and decorated the harnesses with ribbons and paper flowers, vying with each other to win prizes. The carnival parade marched right through Whitley Bay to the Links. There were jazz and pipe bands. After dark, there was a confetti battle – great fun when the boys put handfuls of confetti down the girls' necks. It was all harmless fun in those carefree days before war broke out.

Alice Reynolds's school holiday in Plumpton, a village ten miles from her home in Brighton, stood out in memory.

Kitty and little Alice took the train to Plumpton.

The fish train was in and to combat the smell of fish, we had some eau de cologne-soaked hankies to hold to our noses. I expect the strong smell made Kit feel very queasy.

We arrived at Plumpton at 9pm. It was dusk and an hour past my bedtime (my mum was a great stickler for an 8pm retirement). As we walked up the main street, I could smell a beautiful perfume: it was night-scented stock [a hardy annual with pretty pastel flowers that release scent at night], my first introduction to those flowers.

Kitty's family, the Graingers, lived in a cottage in a secluded laneway.

Kit's mum was quiet and kind and I was able to do as I pleased, which made a change from the upheaval of home. One day, Kit's father took me to Wivelsfield to pick some sphagnum moss – this was to help someone with a child who was wetting the bed. As the moss is very absorbent, it helps keep the bedclothes dry. It was a very long way to walk but it was so interesting because Mr Grainger was able to tell me the names of the flowers and butterflies we saw along the walk.

Another time, Kit's brother Jim took me to pick crab apples to make crab-apple jelly. He shook the tree and little apples rattled down on my head. I cried. Jim laughed, but he was a kind young man and let me carry the basket home.

One day, wandering around, Alice came across a barn with dark green doors left ajar.

I was curious so pushed the door open wider and slipped inside. Two men were in there with a sheep that had been slaughtered and they were in the process of 'dressing it out' as my mother would have called it (in other words, gutting and cleaning it and dividing up the carcass). I was fascinated. There was heart, lungs and the stomach – full of grass – and all the other offal from the animal. The men gave me the sweetbread for my tea and when I gave it to Mrs Grainger to cook, she asked me where I had got it. When I explained what I had seen, everyone was aghast. At first, they felt I should not have seen a sight like that. Then they were amused at the way I had been so interested in what had been going on.

After a glorious, peaceful and free holiday, my mother

and sister arrived to take me home. I cried bitterly, but of course, I had to go!

Peter Pitt's childhood seaside holidays with his parents in the 1930s were carefully organised.

When we went on holiday, our luggage preceded us. We had a trunk more than three feet long, into which my mother would pack clothes for the three of us to cover all weather eventualities.

Locked and tied with a rope, the trunk would then await the luggage carrier, Carter Patterson. They could be contacted at local shops or if you displayed a card with the letters CP in your front window, a passing van would call to collect. The next time you saw your trunk was at your boarding house. Occasionally, things would go wrong. On one holiday, we arrived at the boarding house on Saturday to find that the trunk hadn't come. My father was irate and went back to the railway station to complain. It was delivered on the Monday and at last we were able to change our clothes.

Holiday destinations for the family were Clacton-on-Sea in Essex, Cliftonville in Kent and many South Coast resorts.

The arrangement with some of the boarding houses where we stayed was for the boarders – us – to supply the fish and meat of the main meal of the day. At one establishment, the same hard rock cakes seemed to be dished up at every meal. We used to joke about them for years afterwards.

We spent two holidays at a boarding house in Dundonald Drive, Leigh-on-Sea, where my parents became quite friendly with the landlady, Mrs Long. Sometimes she'd come down to the beach with us with her son, Paul, who was around my age.

On the journey from Dundonald Drive to the beach we had to pass Chalkwell station, where outside on the pavement was a street photographer. He had one of those old wooden movie cameras on a tripod and turned a handle to take a photograph. My parents bought a picture of us walking along the road from him, but he still filmed us every time we passed him.

Every seaside resort had a bandstand. My parents loved to sit and listen to the military bands but as far as I was concerned, we were using up good beach time!

After our holiday was over, clothes, buckets and spades were packed away in the trunk and we travelled home by train. A few days later, the trunk would be delivered to our doorstep.

Londoner Eva Merrill's pre-war family holidays at the seaside were also carefully planned by her father:

He would pay in a weekly sum to a holiday fund. Each June, he would draw out his year's savings, plus a small amount of interest, and we went away for two weeks holiday to the sea. This was an adventure indeed. One year we went to Margate and the next, the Isle of Wight. For some reason these holidays were always alternated, year about.

When we went to Margate we went by the Orange Coach Service – 'charabancs' they were called. We would pick this coach up in Green Lanes [North London] and invariably, nearly always missed it. Last-minute hitches always occurred and we'd be chasing down the road, suitcases, spades and buckets in hand, usually arriving just as the coach was about to take off without us. Once settled on the coach, having got our breath back, the holiday had begun.

At this point Father always put a large white handkerchief, knotted at all four corners, on his head. It looked rather peculiar but somehow this was part of his holiday gear and signalled the start of the holiday. He wore an open-necked shirt and grey flannels with a sports jacket. For a day or so he appeared somewhat awkward in this casual wear and I am sure he missed his formal suit, collar and tie. We had new summer dresses Mother had made, she also had some new hand-made dresses and we all had new hand-knitted cardigans. One always travelled in 'best' clothes in the 1930s and these travelling outfits were always carefully thought out.

On arrival at Margate, we went to our boarding house, the same one every year. We had full board, which meant we were very well looked after. We were given a very filling breakfast, at midday a large cooked dinner was provided, 'high tea' as it was termed arrived at 6pm and we always had a supper snack before going to bed. There were usually about three or four other families staying at the same time and we all sat down together to these meals. We loved Margate, the sands were so beautiful and the weather always seemed kind to us.

The Isle of Wight was also a favourite place. Here again, we stayed at a boarding house with full board. Each Wednesday during the summer months they used to hold competitions and races on the pier. The pier concert hall was packed on these days with well-known comedians and other stars appearing. The audience were encouraged to participate with singing and dancing while the children were organised into various races on the pier.

One Wednesday, they held a laughing competition to find out the holidaymaker with the most infectious laugh. For some reason my mother went up onto the stage along with crowds of other contestants – a most uncharacteristic move on her part for she was usually fairly quiet and somewhat shy. The comedian of the week took them one by one and set them laughing and there was simply no contest! Mother's laugh rang out and, before long, she had the whole audience laughing along with her.

We clapped and cheered. Mother was photographed with the comedian and received a handsome prize. I had won a running race. So, the family came away that Wednesday feeling very pleased with themselves.

The next Wednesday, we went back to try our luck again. A different comedian but he also decided to have a laughing competition, so up again went Mother and repeated the performance. Another photo and another prize, we felt really proud of her.

Simple pleasures in those days, but how we enjoyed ourselves!

For so many, the outbreak of war came while they were in the midst of their annual summer holiday. Doris Jenner, nicknamed 'Jiffi', and her sister had set off on holiday just a week before war broke out.

It was the last Saturday of August 1939 and a lovely summer day as we prepared for our holiday at the seaside. We loaded our luggage and a box of food into the back of Dad's Bedford lorry, then I climbed into the cab, followed by Mum and my younger sister, who had to sit on Mum's lap. Dad checked that the door was fastened securely, then got into the driver's seat. At last we were ready.

We left our village and drove into Sussex. Everywhere was tranquil and beautiful as we travelled to Bishopstone, a small seaside place between Seaford and Newhaven. A relative had a chalet/bungalow there and had invited us to use it. The chalet was one of several built on concrete foundations on the beach, which had originally held army huts during the First World War. It was named 'Lundy' and consisted of two rooms and a verandah.

When we got there, we unloaded the lorry, had a meal on the verandah and then walked to Newhaven Quay to watch the ferry boat arrive from France and the returning holidaymakers disembark. As I watched, I dreamed of visiting Paris the following summer.

We spent a happy weekend playing on the beach, paddling and enjoying meals on the verandah. Dad had to return home on the Sunday evening as he was booked for work with his lorry for the following two days. At that time, his work was spasmodic, so he couldn't afford to refuse any job, but he planned to rejoin us later in the week.

My sister and I continued to enjoy ourselves on the beach, sometimes playing with the dog staying at the next chalet or walking along the sea wall path with Mum to a little shop to buy ice creams.

Although Mum was aware of the threat of war, we had no wireless set or daily newspaper, so we didn't realise how serious the situation was becoming. Each day, we expected Dad to return and when he didn't, we wondered why. The ferry boats continued to go to France and back, although later in the week we were not permitted onto the quay to watch.

As we finished breakfast on the Saturday morning, Dad arrived. But our pleasure quickly turned to dismay when he told us that war was imminent and he had to take us home immediately. He'd been unable to join us sooner as his lorry had been requisitioned by the ARP to take extra first-aid equipment to our local clinic and deliver several hundred sandbags for protecting important buildings in our village. In retrospect, these precautions were premature for at that time our village was considered a safe area and was designated a reception centre for children being evacuated from a London school.

We packed up, tidied the chalet and reluctantly climbed into the lorry once more. The journey back was a sad one, even the countryside seemed sombre. Arriving home, we gathered around the wireless set and listened anxiously. Next morning, war was declared.

We never saw Lundy again as the chalets were demolished during the war but, many years later, I sailed from Newhaven to visit Paris.

My dream belatedly came true.

THE DAY THE WAR ENDED

THERE WOULD BE TIMES OVER THE NEXT FIVE YEARS AND more when, to the British people, it must have seemed that the war would never end; that they would be doomed to live out their lives with rationing, blackouts, shortages of all kind, restrictive regulations, and the constant threat of sudden death. Worse, there were times, too, when it would seem that all was lost, and that the country would be occupied by the tyrannical regime it had fought to destroy, at great cost. But end it did, although nothing would ever be the same again.

Just after midnight on 8 May 1945, a huge storm accompanied by violent thunder and sheets of lightning broke out over London. Some claimed it was the worst storm since the outbreak of the Second World War.

Curiously, in one of nature's grand theatrical gestures, the May storm was virtually a re-run of the big thunderstorm that had swept the country during the night of 2 September 1939, just before war broke out.

Later that day in May, another kind of storm burst forth onto Britain's streets. A very human explosion, if you like, of relief merged with sheer, unadulterated jubilation that the longed-for moment had finally come – 'the day for which the British people have fought and endured five years, eight months and four days of war,' as the *Daily Mirror* described it.

Here was VE Day, Victory in Europe. Two days of public holidays in celebration of victory. The build-up to the day had been a series of events which seemed hardly believable to many, since the war's ending had been anticipated as far back as the previous summer after D-Day, 6 June 1944, which launched the Allied liberation of Western Europe.

On that day, some 156,000 American, British and Canadian forces had landed on a 50-mile stretch along the coast in France's Normandy region. It was one of the largest amphibious military assaults in history. By late August 1944, all of northern France had been liberated from the Nazis. D-Day, or 'Operation Overlord' as it was known, would go down in history as the beginning of the end.

On the afternoon of 30 April 1945, as Russian troops closed in on Berlin, Adolf Hitler committed suicide in a Berlin bunker. The man the newspapers called 'the world's chief criminal' was gone. His death was announced by the BBC in a news flash on the evening of 1 May and in the newspapers the following day.

'His mad dream of a 1,000-year Reich was over at a cost of an estimated thirty million dead, including six million Jews murdered in death and labour camps,' [reported the *Mirror*]. The defeated German nation, which had long lost faith in their deranged Führer, was told he was killed fighting and fell for Germany.' As leading Nazis made an undignified scramble to save their own skins, Hitler's successor, Grand-Admiral Doenitz, ordered the military struggle to continue, but surrender was imminent.

Effectively, the British Army's war in Europe was over at that point. But for several more days, the war on other fronts dragged painfully slowly to its official ending (and the war against the Japanese in the Far East would drag on until August). For everyone, the tension was nigh unbearable, as Joan Strange in Worthing recorded in her diary.

29 APRIL

Rumours of surrenders are still rife. Mussolini has been tried and rumoured shot today. Hitler is supposed to be dying from cerebral haemorrhage. Berlin is nothing but a mass of rubble but terrible fighting continues there. Today's paper says the only purpose of resistance has been to gratify the nihilism of the Nazi chiefs, anxious that, if they must perish, their country shall perish with them.

THE DAY WAR BROKE OUT

1 MAY

It is reported that Count Folke Bernadotte, head of the Swedish Red Cross, has seen Himmler again about the surrender plans but nothing definite has been disclosed. The papers are full of Mussolini's death. He was strung up, head downwards, with his mistress on meat hooks in a petrol station – it all sounds medieval. [Italy, under Fascist dictator Benito Mussolini, had allied itself with Hitler in 1936 and entered the Second World War on Germany's side in June 1940. After Mussolini was ousted in July 1943, Italy signed an unconditional surrender with the Allies in September 1943; Mussolini was executed by Italian partisans on 28 April 1945. The German forces in Italy, however, continued to fight on, forcing the Allies to undertake a succession of hard battles to liberate the country.]

2 MAY

The news is most extraordinary: the Nazi radio late last night announced the death of Hitler, saying, 'He died a hero's death at his post in Berlin.' What can we make of this? Admiral Doenitz takes his place, Himmler seems to have vanished, likewise Goering, Goebbels and von Ribbentrop. [The four principal Nazi leaders were all dead within two years: Hitler, Himmler, Goering and Goebbels committed suicide and von Ribbentrop, sentenced to death at Nuremburg in 1946, was hanged in October 1946.]

Mr Churchill has announced that all resistance in Italy has ended – a magnificent achievement. At 10.30, our wireless was interrupted to tell us that Berlin has fallen to the Russians today. What will happen next? British troops have taken Lubeck and cut off the Nazis in Denmark. Civil Defence has come to an end officially today. [The title ARP, used to describe the civilian Air Raid Precaution services which played such a crucial role throughout the bombing of Britain, was changed to Civil Defence Service in 1941.]

4 MAY

There is a tremendous feeling of repressed excitement as today may be V-Day! Soldiers and helpers all listened in at 9pm at the YMCA canteen to hear the news that all organised resistance by the Nazis in north-west Europe, Denmark, Holland, Heligoland and the Frisian Islands ceases tomorrow at 8am. At 10.30pm, the BBC broke into the programmes to give a recording of the surrender by the Germans to Field Marshal Montgomery at 6.20pm. According to today's paper, the Nazis are trying a 'Dunkirk' and some ships and U-boats are endeavouring to get to Norway but are being harried by the RAF. Queen Wilhelmina is in Holland and there are great scenes of rejoicing already in Holland and Denmark tonight.

5 MAY

Not quite VE Day yet! London is in a terrific state of excitement and expects the announcement at any minute. Fighting continues still in the South, but Russians and Americans are rushing ahead into Czechoslovakia. Sweden seems to think that the Nazis will capitulate in Norway very soon. The seventy-nine passenger stations in the tube systems of London Transport, which have been used as air-raid shelters ever since the first London raids in 1940, will be closed as shelters after tomorrow.

At 2.41am in the early hours of 7 May, at a schoolhouse in Reims, France that served as Supreme Headquarters, Allied Expeditionary Force, General Alfred Jodl signed the unconditional surrender of all German land, sea and air forces, wherever they might be. General Walter Bedell Smith, Chief of Staff to the Allied Supreme Commander, General Dwight D. Eisenhower, signed on behalf of the Allies, and the document was witnessed by generals from France and the Soviet Union. The surrender was to come into effect at 59 minutes to midnight (11:01pm) on 8 May.

'Field Marshal Montgomery and his men have beaten the Hun to his knees along the whole of their front and have written "finis" to the German Reich,' trumpeted the *Daily Mirror*, a declaration which, perhaps understandably, rather overlooked the part played by US and Soviet Russian forces.

In London, where end-of-war excitement was reaching fever pitch, a public announcement of war's end should have been made at 6pm on 7 May. Churchill had alerted the War Cabinet and the Chiefs of Staff (respectively, the political and military bodies with overall responsibility for the war effort) to be ready to go with him to Buckingham Palace. There, he planned to make the official announcement. But the Soviet leader Stalin had other ideas: he insisted that the official surrender of German forces on the Eastern Front must take place in Russian-occupied Berlin with his foremost commander, Marshal Zhukov, as the senior Allied signatory to this and the surrender agreed in Reims. VE Day, Stalin insisted, could not be announced until this happened on 8 May. He wanted the announcement of the end of the war to take place on 9 May, at 7am Moscow time.

Throughout 7 May, frantic communications took place between London, Moscow and Washington. At one stage Churchill rang the Supreme Allied Commander in Western Europe, General Eisenhower, eight times.

Nothing had been agreed about the official announcement when the newly appointed German Foreign Minister threw a giant spanner into the works. Broadcasting from Flensburg in the small area of northern German controlled by the provisional government of Admiral Doenitz, Count Schwerin von Krosigk said that German forces had surrendered and the war was officially over. The broadcast was flashed across the globe and reported, without comment, on BBC News at 3pm on 7 May. Ironically, as the victors argued about the timing of the announcement, it was the defeated who were officially telling the world that the war in Europe had ended.

Then the Paris Bureau Chief of the Associated Press news agency, Edward Kennedy, who, along with sixteen other journalists, had witnessed the historic signing of the surrender at Reims, but had been told to refrain from reporting the news so that Stalin could hold a ceremony in Berlin, decided to defy the news embargo. Via the AP bureau in London, he too reported the surrender, the first Allied journalist to break the story. On the streets of New York, the victory celebrations started as soon as the news broke.

Behind the scenes, however, the day's frantic negotiations between the Allies had reached a stalemate: the Americans were willing to comply with Stalin's request, Churchill was not.

Already that evening, the streets of Central London were thronged with thousands of people impatiently waiting for the official news, ready to celebrate, many dismayed and grumbling at the delay to the announcement, with good reason.

The Ministry of Food had ruled that no extra food would be released to restaurants and the 5-shilling limit on the price of a meal would not be waived. Leading brewers were promising nothing: supplies were low, they said. An extension of pub hours was unlikely. It seemed like a mean-spirited prelude to the celebration millions had dreamed of.

Finally, a compromise was reached that evening of 7 May: the people would be told immediately that Tuesday, 8 May would be Victory in Europe day, while on the following day, 9 May, Britain's 'Great Russian Ally' would be celebrating its own VE Day: both days would be public holidays.

That morning of 8 May, the early editions of the UK papers headlined the news everyone had been waiting for: 'IT'S ALL OVER!' stated the *Daily Mail*. 'VE-DAY! IT'S OVER IN THE WEST,' said the *Mirror*, in a rare reference to the continuing war in the Far East. A report from one of its journalists in London's Piccadilly Circus at just after midnight enthused:

> We are all going nuts! We are dancing the conga and the jig and 'Knees Up Mother Brown'. We are singing and whistling and blowing paper trumpets. The idea is to make a noise. Gangs of girls and soldiers of all the Allied nations are waving rattles and shouting and climbing lamp-posts, swarming over cars that have become bogged down in this struggling, swirling mass of celebrating Londoners.
>
> A paper-hatted throng is trying to pull me out of this telephone box now. I hold the door tight, but the din is drowning my voice.

Mollie Panter-Downes was an English novelist and journalist who wrote a series of vividly perceptive articles about London life in wartime for *The New Yorker* magazine. Here is her description of London celebrating the end of war in Europe:

THE DAY WAR BROKE OUT

When the day finally came it was like no other day that anyone can remember. It had a flavour of its own, an extemporaneousness which gave it something of the quality of a vast, happy village fête as people wandered about, sat, sang and slept against a slimmer background of trees, grass, flowers and water. Apparently the desire to assist in London's celebration combusted spontaneously in the bosom of every member of every family, from the smallest babies, with their hair done up in red, white and blue ribbons, to beaming elderly couples who, utterly without self-consciousness, strolled up and down the streets, arm in arm in red, white and blue paper hats. Even the dogs wore immense tricoloured bows. The bells had begun to peal and, after the night's storm, London was having that perfect, hot, English summer's day which, one sometimes feels, is to be found only in the imaginations of the lyric poets.

The girls in their thin, bright dresses heightened the impression that the city had been taken over by an enormous family picnic. The number of extraordinarily pretty young girls, who presumably are hidden on working days inside the factories and government offices, was astonishing. Strolling with their uniformed boys, arms candidly about each other, they provided a constant, gay, simple marginal decoration to the big solemn moments of the day.

The crowds milled back and forth between the Palace, Westminster, Trafalgar Square and Piccadilly Circus and when they got tired, they simply sat down wherever they happened to be – on the grass, on doorsteps or on the kerb –

and watched the other people or spread handkerchiefs over their faces and took a nap. Everybody appeared determined to see the King and Queen and Mr Churchill at least once, and few could have been disappointed.

By lunchtime, in the Circus, the buses had to slow to a crawl in order to get through the tightly packed, laughing people. A lad in the black beret of the Tank Corps was the first to climb the little pyramidal Angkor Wat of scaffolding and sandbags which was erected early in the war to protect the pedestal of the Eros statue after the figure had been removed to safekeeping. The boy shinned up to the top and took a tiptoe Eros pose, aiming an imaginary bow, while the crowd roared.

He was followed by a paratrooper in a maroon beret, who, after getting up to the top, reached down and hauled up a young blonde woman in a very tight pair of green slacks. When she got to the top, the Tank Corps soldier promptly grabbed her in his arms and, encouraged by ecstatic cheers from the whole Circus, seemed about to enact the classic role of Eros right on the top of the monument. Nothing came of it, because a moment later, a couple of GIs joined them and before long, the pyramid was covered with boys and girls.

They sat jammed together in an affectionate mass, swinging their legs over the sides, wearing each other's uniform caps and calling down wisecracks to the crowd.

'My God,' someone said, 'think of a flying bomb coming down on this!' When a firecracker went off, a hawker with a tray of tin brooches of Monty's [Field Marshal Montgomery's] head happily yelled that comforting, sometimes fallacious phrase of the Blitz nights, 'All right, mates, it's one of ours!'

All day long, the deadly past was for most people only just under the surface of the beautiful, safe present, so much so that the Government decided against sounding the sirens in a triumphant 'all clear' for fear that the noise would revive too many painful memories.

For the same reason, there were no salutes of guns – only the pealing of the bells and the whistles of tugs on the Thames sounding the doot, doot, doot, doooot of the 'V' [for victory; 3 short, 1 long in Morse code] and the roar of the planes, which swooped back and forth over the city, dropping red and green signals toward the blur of smiling, upturned faces.

It was without any doubt, Churchill's day. Thousands of King George's subjects wedged themselves in front of the Palace throughout the day, chanting ceaselessly, 'We want the King' and cheering themselves hoarse when he and the Queen and their daughters appeared, but when the crowd saw Churchill, there was a deep, full-throated, almost reverent roar. He was at the head of a procession of Members of Parliament, walking back to the House of Commons from the traditional St Margaret's Thanksgiving Service [St Margaret's Church, Westminster, on Parliament Square, was until 1972 the Anglican parish church of the House of Commons]. Instantly, he was surrounded by people – people running, standing on tiptoe, holding up babies so that they could be told later they had seen him and shouting affectionately the absurd little nurserymaid name 'Winnie, Winnie!' One or two happily sozzled, very old and incredibly dirty Cockneys who had been engaged in a slow, shuffling dance, like a couple of Shakespearean clowns, bellowed, 'That's 'im, that's 'is little old lovely bald 'ead!' American sailors and laughing girls formed a conga line down the middle of Piccadilly and Cockneys linked arms in the Lambeth Walk.

It was a day and night of no fixed plan and no organised merriment. Each group danced its own dance, sang its own song, and went on its own way as the spirit moved it. The most tolerant, self-effacing people in London on VE Day were the police, who simply stood by, smiling benignly, while soldiers swung by one arm from lamp standards and laughing groups tore down hoardings to build the evening's bonfires. The young servicemen and women who swung arm in arm down the middle of every street, singing and swarming over the few cars rash enough to come out, were simply happy with an immense holiday happiness. They were the liberated people who, like their counterparts in every celebrating capital that night, were young enough to outlive the past and to look forward to an unspoilt future.

Their gaiety was very moving.

There were, of course, street parties all over the country on VE Day, though many more took place over the succeeding weeks. Rationing made it difficult but, none-theless, women managed somehow to get together the sandwiches, cakes, trifles, biscuits and lemonade to give the children a good time for their Victory tea party.

Frank Mee was working as an apprentice at a large engineering firm in Stockton-on-Tees, County Durham, on VE Day. He was sixteen years old.

We all knew it was coming. A couple of the men I worked with had been in the Army after D-Day, wounded, sent home and then invalided out, so we got some idea of what it was like for those still fighting. Then the news came that we'd be getting a day off work for the official VE Day, 8 May.

Mother, as did many people, dived into her War Stock, the secret supply put away for what was to come but never did. The tins of fruit, Carnation milk, a large tin of Del Monte peaches, goodies that had come in wooden boxes every six months or so from family in New Zealand. Dad opened the garage doors and set out tables and chairs from the loft above the stables; people congregated, bringing food, cake and goodies, and we had an ad-hoc street party.

Later, all us young ones congregated on Norton Green and watched the older ones as hidden bottles of drink came from nowhere and were consumed. Long-hidden bottles of sherry appeared and Green Goddess cocktail, a horrible concoction my mother loved and had hidden for years. There was a happy air about it all as if we were all suddenly able to fly, more food was eaten and us youngsters set off walking into town to go dancing. The dance hall had opened its doors. It was free, although trying to dance was impossible – it was so riotous with flags draped around the hall and lights full on. So, we set off back home, dancing, singing and kissing everyone we met – well, I drew the line at hairy-faced sailors – but a few grans got kissed. Back onto the Green and we found a huge bonfire at the top of Beaconsfield Street with crowds around it.

The party went on until well into the night. Someone had put a couple of sacks of potatoes into the ashes of the fire. Others brought butter and cheese for the potatoes and there seemed to be gallons of drink. A lot of the older folk, for whom this was the second Victory Day in just less than thirty years, let their hair down. Sometime around one in the morning, with the bonfire down to embers and a girl in my arms who was not exactly saying: 'Don't do that!', I thought my life was made until a stentorian voice yelling, 'Come on, Mary! Time for bed!' interrupted my dreams. Oh well, it was probably for the best. And so the day ended. We all knew of the girl down the road who was sent away to have her baby – she swore blind she'd only been kissing. We boys still only guessed at the mechanics of all that kind of thing.

We woke next morning to see the papers covered with pictures of the crowds in London all going mad. As we sat down to our usual breakfast, porridge, sugar and milk, then bacon and egg and fried bread – we had not suffered as city dwellers had as we had our own smallholding – Dad looked at me and said: 'We have the Japanese to finish yet and that will be a long haul, you could end up in this war yet.' He was not to know it was my most ardent wish. I wanted to be in there with the Army and not skulking about at home. He hoped it was over before they wanted me, daft as I was. I did go much later and find my own little war and he was right, you do not volunteer for that kind of thing twice.

We all got back to work a day later and were standing around chatting about what we had done when the boss came in and shouted: 'Okay, you lot, back to work, the bloody war is not over yet!' Little did we know that the USA was preparing Armageddon for the Japanese and the rest of the world would live under its cloud for the next fifty years.

For a couple of days, we rejoiced, felt free and uplifted, enjoyed it all, then back into the grist mill. From my experience it settled nothing – but we were not to know that.

Where I lived, we'd had nearly three years of night raids, some heavy bombing, people killed, property destroyed. Now it had gone, we thought the good times were coming. Only they did not: it got worse. Things were rationed that had not been rationed in the war, the austerity years, so our war seemed never-ending. But rationing ended in 1954, house building started, and there was plenty of work for those wanting it.

By 1947, I was in the Army and still able to smell a dance hall twenty miles away. Yet the war had shaped my life and my future. It was exciting, frightening and very funny in turns, the pace of living had increased as we came to a day-to-day style of doing things, the cry being 'We might not be here tomorrow.' That was only half said in jest. And it took us a long time to get back to a normal life.

I pray for my grandchildren's sake it never happens again.

As Frank Mee outlined, the VE Day celebrations had a dramatic and totally unexpected finale. The war with Japan was expected to go on for a year or so, but the dropping of the atomic bombs on Hiroshima and Nagasaki by the Americans at the beginning of August 1945 changed everything. On the morning of 15 August, it was announced that the Japanese had surrendered unconditionally and VJ Day celebrations began; the Second World War officially ended on 2 September 1945.

Events in Britain proved equally unexpected. On 26 July, the nation's beloved wartime 'Winnie', Winston Churchill, had been forced to resign as Prime Minister, following the Conservative Party's defeat in the first general election held in Britain for more than a decade. On the same day, the leader of the Labour Party, Clement Attlee, became the country's new leader. Attlee's victory represented huge social change ahead: it would usher in the formation of the welfare state and the birth of the National Health Service for Britain. Yet as far as war's ending was concerned, the meeting between 'The Big Three' Allied powers, heads of state, Harry S. Truman, Joseph Stalin and Winston Churchill at the Potsdam Conference in Germany from 17 July to 2 August 1945, where it was hoped the key issues of the international post-war world would be resolved, was clouded by an atmosphere of suspicion and unease.

Stalin was initially unwilling to negotiate the future of those Eastern European countries then occupied by Soviet forces. In due course, the negotiation would lead to huge swaths of Europe remaining more or less under Soviet control until 1991.

Churchill, already on edge about the result of the general election, had to leave the conference on 26 July for the election result – and his place at Potsdam was taken, days later, by the new British Prime Minister Clement Attlee.

It was a huge shock. Britain had undoubtedly loved and respected its wartime warrior, but the country yearned for change. When Churchill's leading physician, Lord Moran, criticised the ingratitude of the nation, Churchill's response was typically astute: 'Oh no,' he said. 'I wouldn't call it that. They have had a very hard time.'

Truman, for his part, had only recently become the American President. In April 1945, less than a month before Hitler took his own life, President Franklin D. Roosevelt had died, so consigning to history his important personal friendship with Churchill during the war years. Truman, formerly Roosevelt's Vice-President, had very serious preoccupations during the Potsdam talks. In total secrecy, he signed off on the subsequent use of the atomic bomb on the Japanese cities Hiroshima and Nagasaki on

6 and 9 August. He was unaware that, by then, Stalin had his own nuclear agenda: the Soviets were already in the process of developing their own atomic weapons.

The conference achieved agreement on the status of demilitarised Germany, splitting it into four separate occupation zones, controlled by the US, Britain, France and the Soviet Union. But mostly, in historical terms, it was a marker to the end of the power of the British Empire – and the beginning of the Cold War. By August 1949, the Soviets had detonated their first atomic bomb. The nuclear arms race, which was to dominate global politics through the 1950s and beyond, was well under way.

Six years of war had left the country with huge overseas debts, rundown industry and an acute housing shortage, with almost a third of all houses damaged by bombs. For millions of women like Megan Ryan, VE Day and its celebration was a time for reflection. That day, her twenty-sixth birthday, she had learned that her husband, Peter, in hospital, was out of danger.

That evening, after the children were asleep in bed, I went outside and sat on the low front wall before the house – the wall from which the ornamental iron railings had long since been taken for the war effort. It was a warm, still evening and the long street was quiet. But from almost every window light streamed out, splashing onto the pavement. Curtains had been pulled aside and blackouts had been removed. For the first time in nearly six years we were released from the necessity of hiding out in darkness and people were reacting by letting the lights from their home shine out.

Too tired to move, I sat thinking about those six years. When they began, I'd been twenty, full of enthusiasms, ambitions, certainties and energy of youth. I'd married, borne children, but the war had stolen from us the simple ordinary joys of a young couple shaping a shared life.

Our first home had been burnt to rubble and with it had gone many of the gifts which relatives and friends had given us and which should have been treasured for life, while what had been salvaged would always bear the marks of that night of destruction. We had known the agony of separation and the too rare, too short, too heightened joys of reunions. Apart, we had endured illnesses and dangers and fears for each other. As a family, too, we had been separated and now must learn to live together, overcoming the barriers set up by experiences which had not been shared.

I thought of those who had been dear to us who had not lived to see this. Of John, who had stood at the altar with us on our wedding day, John who had been trapped in his cockpit when his plane sank beneath the waves. Of Ron, constant companion of my brother since schooldays, who had vanished without trace when the troopship he was on had been sunk by the Japanese. Of Peter, my girlhood friend's gay, kind brother, who had been shot while trying to escape from the prisoner-of-war camp to which he had been taken. They were all so young. The youngest died at nineteen, the oldest at twenty-four. I sat thinking of them and then went indoors to stand looking at the sleeping faces of my two little boys, whose lives lay before them in a world at peace.

Philip C. Gunyon, survivor of the sinking of the *Athenia* on the day war broke out, was living with his family in Oakville, Toronto, on VE Day. He had just turned thirteen.

I was just completing my first year in Grade 9 at Oakville High School. We didn't get the day off, but there was a sense of closure, knowing that Hitler was dead and that his armies had been vanquished on the Eastern and Western Fronts. I had followed these stories during 1944 and there was a sense of relief that it was over now. But over only in Europe. We still had the Japs to finish off and our neighbouring Americans were still doing so at a frightful cost. I was wondering how long it would take for the other shoe to drop.

My dad had spent many years in Japan for his English firm, Mather and Platt, and he had joined the Royal Canadian Navy, Special Branch, as an interpreter and had been sent to Australia and, eventually, Shanghai to interrogate Japanese prisoners. So, I was wondering when he'd get home. [Eventually, in 1946.] But on that day in May, I was thinking too about a girl in my class whose big brother now lay in a grave in Holland and I remembered the Remembrance Sundays in November during the war, when the names of the other Oakville men who had been killed were read out in St Jude's Church, where we went every Sunday.

In the city centre of Toronto, VE Day was celebrated by a jubilant crowd intent on enjoying themselves. However, in Philip's quiet suburb, twenty-five miles outside the city, there were no big street parties for the 5,000 or so inhabitants.

'There was only a sense of relief and thanksgiving.'

The conflict had been total war. It had involved and affected everyone in Britain. High taxes, conscription, food and other rationing and many shortages, as well as air raids on many cities and the all-encompassing government regulations and restrictions. No one in the country could avoid war's effect.

How much hardship and tragedy each family endured can never be calculated or assessed. The Second World War's toll of 400,000 British people killed was, in fact, lower than the 750,000 who had been killed in the First World War – which had lasted one year less.

As already described, when war broke out in 1939, the immediate impact was not, as anticipated, a swift aerial bombardment. Instead, the true impact on the civilian population took place gradually: month by month, year by year.

EPILOGUE: THE DAY WAR ENDED

Food rationing began in January 1940. Then the events of April to June 1940 brought harsher circumstances. After 10 May 1940, when German forces started to overwhelm Belgium, Holland and France, the real impact of war on Britain's civilian population started to take hold.

The Dunkirk Evacuation of 338,226, British, French and Belgian troops from the beaches of Dunkirk, France, by a hastily assembled fleet of 800 vessels, comprising Royal Navy and French warships, civilian merchant ships, fishing boats, steamers, river cruisers, and even small sailing craft was heralded as a 'miracle', a triumph over adversity, a heroic rescue mission against the odds.

Nonetheless, the story of the evacuation of Dunkirk on 3 June 1940 assumed the proportions of a victory of sorts, mostly thanks to the courageous efforts of hundreds of ordinary people who determinedly set sail to participate in the rescue.

The Battle of Britain: Nearly a year after war began came the Battle of Britain and the German aerial attempt to destroy the Royal Air Force prior to an invasion of England, which aside from bombing raids on cities, saw a concerted assault on Britain's airfields and radar stations in southern England. It lasted from 10 July to 15 September. The scale of the Luftwaffe attack was huge, but the country's defences – thanks to the efforts of the RAF, backed up by advanced radar and efficient anti-aircraft defences, and underpinned by the pre-war decision to begin production of the much-needed modern fighters, the Spitfire and Hurricane – held firm. There were heavy losses, especially of pilots, but in the final tally, the Luftwaffe came off worse. There is still debate about how serious Hitler was in planning Operation Sealion, the invasion of southern Britain, but with the RAF and the Royal Navy – then the most powerful maritime force in the world – still operational, any such attempt would have been blasted off the surface of the English Channel.

The Blitz (September 1940 to May 1941): the large-scale, nightly air attacks on Britain's cities gave millions of civilians their most severe and bitter taste of war.

London was first, with severe bombing raids every night for two months, then came the aerial assaults on Coventry, Birmingham, Manchester, Liverpool, Bristol, Southampton, Plymouth and other cities. Some thirty thousand people were killed and many more injured, close to four million houses were ruined or damaged. At this point, a second wave of evacuation from London began, though many opted to remain, some in essential voluntary roles as firemen, air-raid wardens or ambulance drivers. (A government programme of factory dispersal in 1940 meant that factory production, so crucial in wartime, was not harmed dramatically. Moreover, factory managers and workers were resolute in their determination to just get on with the job and 'do their bit'.)

Smaller-scale 'tip-and-run' air raids continued after the Blitz. Damaging retaliatory raids on towns like Bath, York and Canterbury, called 'Baedeker raids' (after the popular series of German travel guides published by Baedeker) because of their historic or cultural value, took place in April and May 1942, and would continue sporadically over the next two years.

The V1s and V2s: The most serious resumption of enemy air raids came not long after D-Day in June 1944, when the Germans began to launch the deadly V1 flying bombs, pilotless aircraft that dropped to earth when their engines cut out, detonating an 1,800-pound warhead.

In September that year, the V2 rockets – the world's first long-range ballistic missiles – were launched against London and South-East England, killing 10,000 people and bringing a renewed evacuation of London. These lethal weapons were also used towards the end of the war in Belgium, France and the Netherlands. Unlike the V1s – numbers of which were destroyed by fighters or anti-aircraft fire – they could not be seen or heard in flight, and they carried a larger warhead of 2,200 pounds.

Only when the launching sites in Northern France and Belgium were finally overrun by Allied forces in March 1945, mere weeks before hostilities in Europe finally ended, did their use cease.

The foregoing describes, very briefly, the brutal effect of the Second World War on Britain's civilian population. The emotional impact, however, reached far beyond the bombed-out homes in cities and towns. The upheaval of war brought massive disruption to everyday family life. It broke up everything, families and entire neighbourhoods.

Many of those who had been bombed out had to change

their address time and again. From September 1939 to the end of 1945, there were sixty million changes of address across the country – out of a civilian population of thirty-eight million. Housing conditions, family separation, sudden news of the loss of loved ones and the effect of women's mobilisation placed enormous and long-lasting strain on wartime families.

In September 1939, few had believed that women would be called up to go into the forces. At the end of 1941, conscription for women was introduced (though women would not be fighting in combat). By mid-1943, 90 per cent of single women and 80 per cent of married women were engaged in some kind of war work.

Many women had to leave their homes to work elsewhere, specifically in munitions or armaments factories in different parts of the country. For a population where mobility for working people had been quite limited by today's standards, such upheaval brought its own terrors, especially for younger, unmarried women, knowing little outside their immediate environment, but finding themselves working a fifty-five-hour factory week alongside strangers. Those strangers, however, might include young childless women already widowed by war's impact. Evacuation too, as we have seen, would carry a long-lasting emotional impact down the years.

Yet the spirit of the people, for all the deprivation and heartache, remained mostly intact in those years after September 1939. Millions had carried out war work on a purely voluntary basis, despite the blackouts, the rationing and shortages, the shelters and the bombs. Men and women of those times, when interviewed, always, without fail, refer to their absolute pride in 'doing their bit' for their country. The stakes were of the highest order: survival against the odds. Yet there is little question that the nation's inherent qualities – the quiet reserve, the stoicism and the humour, still regarded as very British traits – enabled so many to navigate their way through the worst.

The author J. B. Priestley summed up the mood of the times when he wrote:

> The British were absolutely at their best in the Second World War. They were never so good in my lifetime before it and I'm sorry to say that they've never been so good after it.

RECOMMENDED READING

Brown, Mike, *Evacuees: Evacuation in Wartime Britain 1939–1945*, new edn, History Press, 2005

Gardiner, Juliet, *Wartime Britain 1939–1945*, Headline, 2005

Horn, Pamela, *Behind the Counter: Shop Lives from Market Stall to Supermarket*, reprint edn, Amberley Publishing, 2015

Pugh, Martin, *We Danced All Night: Britain Between the Wars*, Vintage, 2009

Storey, Joyce and Pat Thorne (ed.), *The House in South Road*, Virago, 2004

Waller, Maureen, *London 1945*, new edn, John Murray, 2005

Ziegler, Philip, *London at War 1939–1945*, Pimlico, 2002

SOURCES AND BIBLIOGRAPHY

CHAPTER 2

Excerpts from Constance Miles's diaries, taken from Miles, Constance and Partington, S. V. (ed.), *Mrs Miles's Diary: The Wartime Journal of a Housewife on the Home Front*, London, Simon & Schuster, 2013

Excerpts from Joan Strange's diary, taken from Strange, Joan and McCooey, Chris (ed.), *Despatches from the Home Front: The War Diaries of Joan Strange*, Tunbridge Wells, Jak Books, 1989; new edn 2013

Excerpts from Eva Merrill's memoir: Merrill, Eva, *Looking Back: Reflections of a London Child in the War Years 1939 –1945*, AuthorHouse Publishing, 2013

Excerpts from Everett, Alan, *Corned Beef City: An Autobiography of a Kid from Dagenham*, Kindle edition

CHAPTER 3

Excerpts from Katie Owen taken from author's personal interview

Excerpts from Irene Watts taken from author's personal interview

CHAPTER 4

Excerpts from Ken and Maureen Hone taken from author's personal interview

Excerpts from Molly Rose taken from author's personal interview

Excerpts from Vera Barber taken from author's personal interview

Excerpts from Christine Haig taken from author's personal interview

Excerpts from Jean Ledger taken from author's personal interview

Excerpts from Eileen Weston taken from author's personal interview

Excerpts from Frank Mee taken from author's personal interview

Excerpts from Stella Broughton taken from author's personal interview

Excerpts from Philip Gunyon taken from author's personal correspondence

CHAPTER 5

Excerpts from Merrill, Eva, *Looking Back: Reflections of a London Child in the War years 1939–1945*, AuthorHouse Publishing, 2013

CHAPTER 6

Excerpts from Betty Nettle taken from author's personal interview

Excerpts from Maisie Jagger taken from author's personal interview

Excerpts from Storey, Joyce and Thorne, Pat (ed.), *The House in South Road*, London, Virago, 2004

Excerpts from Reynolds, Alice, *A Penny for the Gas: The personal history of a nonagenarian*, Somerset, Railway Cat Creations, 2011

CHAPTER 7

Excerpts from Frank Mee taken from author's personal interview

Excerpts from Storey, Joyce and Thorne, Pat (ed.), *The House in South Road*, London, Virago, 2004

CHAPTER 8

Excerpts from Frank Mee taken from author's personal interview

Excerpts from Merrill, Eva, *Looking Back: Reflections of a London Child in the War years 1939–1945*, AuthorHouse Publishing, 2013

Excerpts from Reynolds, Alice, *A Penny for the Gas: The personal history of a nonagenarian*, Somerset, Railway Cat Creations, 2011

CHAPTER 9

Excerpts from Frank Mee taken from author's personal interview

Excerpts from Joan Strange's diary, taken from Strange, Joan and McCooey, Chris (ed.), *Despatches from the Home Front: The War Diaries of Joan Strange*, Tunbridge Wells, Jak Books, 1989; new edn 2013

Panter-Downes, Mollie, *London War Notes*, 1971; new edn London, Persephone Books, 2015

OTHER SOURCES
see also Recommended Reading, p.287

de Courcy, Anne, *1939: The Last Season*, new edn Weidenfeld & Nicolson, 2003

Gardiner, Juliet, *Memories of Britain Past: The illustrated story of how we lived, worked and played*, Reader's Digest, 2011

Kynaston, David, *Austerity Britain 1945–51*, reprint edn, Bloomsbury, 2008

SOURCES AND BIBLIOGRAPHY

Longmate, Norman, *How We Lived Then: A History of Everyday Life During the Second World War*, new edn, Pimlico, 2002

—, *The Home Front: An Anthology of Personal Experience 1938–45*, Chatto & Windus, 1981

Miller, Russell: *VE Day: The People's Story*, new edn, History Press, 2007

Nicholson, Virginia, *Millions Like Us: Women's Lives During the Second World War*, Penguin, 2012

Pearce, Robert, *1930s Britain*, Shire Publications, 2010

Smith, May, *These Wonderful Rumours!: A Young Schoolteacher's Wartime Diaries 1939–1945*, Virago, 2013

Waller, Maureen, *A Family in Wartime: How the Second World War shaped the lives of a generation*, Conway, 2012

Yorke, Trevor, *The 1930s House Explained*, reprint edn, Countryside Books, 2006

Backyard Brighton, Selma Montford; there is also a book, *Backyard Brighton: New memories, reflections and photographs* by Jacqueline Pollard, published by Brighton Books in 2007

BBC WW2 People's War online archive (www.bbc.co.uk/history/ww2peopleswar/)

Best of British magazine (www.bestofbritishmag.co.uk/) and Yesterday Remembered (https://yesterdayremembered.co.uk/)

www.1900s.org.uk/ 'Everyday Life, early-mid 20th century, by people who were there'

Daily Telegraph

Derby Telegraph (formerly *Derby Evening Telegraph*)
The Imperial War Museum, London (www.iwm.org.uk/)
London Borough of Barking and Dagenham Archives
   and Local Studies Centre
Mass Observation Archive, Brighton

el/